DECISION MAKING IN THE LEADERSHIP CHAIR

DECISION MAKING IN THE LEADERSHIP CHAIR

Vital Lessons from Visionary Executives

WILLIAM P. LAUDER

Published in the United States by Disruption Books.

ISBN 978-1-63331-002-5

Printed in the United States of America

Design by Studio Kudos

First Edition

WITH

Laura Alber
Michael Berland
Edward D. Breen
Michael Eisner
William Clay Ford, Jr.
Fabrizio Freda
Alex Gorsky
Mellody Hobson
Governor Jon M. Huntsman, Jr.
Jon M. Huntsman, Sr.
Nancy Koehn, Ph.D.
Indra K. Nooyi
Sarah Robb O'Hagan
Richard D. Parsons
James D. Robinson, IV
Dr. Judith Rodin
Arthur O. Sulzberger, Jr.
Michael Useem, Ph.D.
Lauren Zalaznick
Strauss Zelnick

"The wealth of a company is its people."

— *Leonard A. Lauder*

FOREWORD:
LEARNING TO LEAD FROM THE INSIDE

Michael Useem, Ph.D.
The Wharton School of the University of Pennsylvania

For those aspiring to lead an enterprise, few more instructive sources are available than watching those individuals who are already doing so. By witnessing how they have led, we can acquire useful, battle-tested ideas on how we should lead. And since those ideas are rooted in the tangible experiences of individuals with a proven leadership record, they come with exceptional authority.

A great deal of executive leadership is exercised behind closed doors, largely invisible to almost everybody outside the C-suite or the boardroom. Learning directly from the experience of others in the executive suite thus depends on veteran executives who are willing to candidly share their acquired wisdom with those on the outside.

Fortunately, William P. Lauder has worked to open those doors, starting with his own service as Chief Executive Officer and then Executive Chairman of The Estée Lauder Companies. He has also persuaded a host of other executives who have likewise served in a "leadership chair" to report how they have led their own enterprises.

Taken together, they offer a pragmatic and compelling road map for leading an enterprise, whatever the industry. A number of leadership principles emerge, and many of them can be grouped together into three instructive categories: developing and inspiring; leveraging and preparing; and spearheading change.

DEVELOPING AND INSPIRING

Soon after he became Executive Chairman, William and I were comparing calendars over breakfast near the campus of the University of

Pennsylvania, trying to find a mutually agreeable time for a future meeting. I thought I was busy, but I was stunned to learn of his own nearly wall-to-wall commitments stretching out months ahead. Still, he found extra time that morning when I asked him if he might want to accompany me to a 9:00 a.m. course with sixty-five first-year MBA students.

Our topic was managing people at work, and midway through the class I asked William, then comfortably seated in the back row of a tiered classroom, if he would step to the front to tell the class how he managed the thousands who worked for him at The Estée Lauder Companies. It was, he told the students, a matter of first appreciating and then bringing out the best in each person working for him, rather than trying to impose one standard leadership model on all of them. Coming from an experienced denizen of top management, the point hit home with the students and with me. Academic research had amply confirmed the idea, but now it was coming directly from a successful executive who had included it among his first principles for leading his enterprise.

And successful his enterprise has been. William P. Lauder served as CEO of The Estée Lauder Companies from 2004 to 2009, and since then he has served as Executive Chairman, a full-time position in active partnership with President and CEO Fabrizio Freda. Founded in 1946 by William's grandparents, The Estée Lauder Companies has emerged as the premier global player in prestige beauty. In FY 2014, the Company employed more than forty thousand and drew nearly $11 billion in annual revenue.

One of the foundations for the Company's growth, as we learned that day in my class—and now in William's own course at Wharton, as well as in this volume—is developing and inspiring others to do what you should not be doing yourself. Good leadership, he explained, "is all about teaching others to be really good at what they do so that you can do more."

Equally important has been the recruitment of those who *can* do it themselves, and for that William has insisted that his company hire the best talent. As a case in point, he noted that he brought in a seasoned and successful executive from Procter & Gamble, Fabrizio Freda, to succeed him as President and CEO. Since then, Freda's leadership of the Company has had much to do with the firm's increase in market value. Under his direction, concluded a *Fortune* reporter, the Company has become "arguably the top performer in global cosmetics."[1]

LEVERAGING AND PREPARING

Bringing the best out of those who report to you and their subordinates is vital for leveraging any enterprise. But for those sitting in the leadership chair, there is, alas, no simple device for doing so. After all, the chair itself is usually just an office with a telephone, computer, and several staff assistants. Mobilizing hundreds and even thousands of people in a way that consistently aligns their actions with the company's goals and strategy becomes an abiding challenge for anybody in the leadership chair.

Richard D. Parsons had repeatedly confronted just that in two leadership positions, first as chief executive of the multimedia company AOL–Time Warner and then as board chair of America's largest financial institution, Citigroup. The first experience was not a pretty one, as he had become CEO just after AOL and Time Warner merged in what proved to be one of the most disastrous combinations in business history, resulting in a loss of more than $50 billion in shareholder value in a single quarter. Still, he had to move the enterprise forward, and that

---

1   Shawn Tully, "An Outsider in the Family Castle," *Fortune,* October 31, 2013, http://fortune.com/2013/10/31/an-outsider-in-the-family-castle/.

entailed refocusing his staff away from the public debacle and toward the immediate task of integrating the two companies. He worked energetically, he reported, to refocus employees on their own work products instead of the crisis swirling around them. He accomplished this by first defining the company reality with which they should be most concerned, and then by generating optimism that everybody would be able to get their jobs done within that reality.

Harvard Business School historian Nancy Koehn emphasizes the same imperative for anybody in a leadership chair. In a colorful characterization of the challenge, Koehn quotes novelist David Foster Wallace, describing successful leaders as those who "help us overcome the limitations of our own individual laziness and selfishness and weakness and fear and get us to do better, harder things than we can get ourselves to do on our own." To move employees beyond their own limitations, Koehn has found that the best leaders articulate a compelling mission and then help each individual appreciate their unique role in fulfilling that transcendent purpose.

Building a great team and keeping that team energized are also vital leadership tasks, underscores Lauren Zalaznick, an entrepreneur, producer, and executive at large media companies who oversaw numerous cable channels and ushered in innovation and integration initiatives at NBCUniversal. "Every leader relies on a team," she found, "but great leaders empower their teams." Michael Eisner, who held the leadership chair at the Walt Disney Company for two decades, points to the particular importance of building teams across company divisions, through which he often found great synergies. One method for achieving that: Eisner would arrange for twenty senior people from diverse parts of the business to travel for eight days together to see the company's far-flung facilities. In the process, they would learn as much about one another's operations as they did about the sites they visited.

James D. Robinson, IV, co-founder and managing partner of the technology-focused venture capital firm RRE Ventures, warns of the importance of knowing how to effectively communicate your leadership directives. Working with partners, he found, required greater sensitivity to their special interests and concerns. Robinson worried, for instance, about the potential reaction of a partner if he opposed the partner's investment proposal without a compelling rationale for the resistance. Unless Robinson thoughtfully explained his opposition, he feared that the partner might subsequently oppose one of his recommended venture investments. Leading the firm requires an exquisite appreciation for how people perceive—and thus are willing to accept— one's decisions and direction.

It is often noted that you cannot take the lead if you have not worked to prepare yourself for the leadership chair. This requires physical and mental stamina for the long hours and grueling demands, but it also requires an appreciation for how you can best lead. Michael Berland, chief executive of a division of Edelman PR, one of the world's leading public communications firms, reminds us from his own experience that you have to appreciate your own animating forces: "You have to understand what it is that motivates you and then use that knowledge to drive your performance."

Johnson & Johnson Chief Executive Alex Gorsky affirms the enduring importance of personal readiness: "My advice is to take care of yourself and your health. In today's environment, the pace, the pressure, the challenges, and all the travel involved in leading a company can take a significant toll on you as an individual. And in the end, who we are as an individual is who we are as a leader. The healthier and more energetic you are as a person, the better you will be at your job."

SPEARHEADING CHANGE

Spearheading change is a third arena that those included in this volume recurrently stress as central to their work in the leadership chair. And changing the enterprise before it needs to change is a top priority for most. "You need to ask yourself," William P. Lauder urges, "do you wither and die to protect the existing business model, or do you take a proactive approach to adapt on your own terms before change becomes necessary?"

The Estée Lauder Companies President and CEO Fabrizio Freda also presses the case for preemptively acting before you are forced to do so. Your future business "will be dramatically different from the past," he warns, and to prepare now, "you have to decide where you want to go and then reverse engineer your success." To do that, he reports, no barrier or crisis can be allowed to get in the way, and thus personal fortitude is an essential ingredient.

Freda would know: he took the helm at The Estée Lauder Companies soon after the United States' and much of the world's economy plunged into recession in the wake of Lehman's and AIG's failures in September 2008. Instead of hunkering down and waiting for a better day to commence his reengineering of the firm, Freda decided to plunge full speed ahead, using the crisis not to excuse the Company's declining sales but instead to accelerate the strategic changes he had already decided were critical for sustaining sales growth in the future.

Among Freda's changes was a strengthening of the Company's partnerships with major retailers in Europe. Rather than allowing finger pointing when revenue sharply dropped in the wake of the 2008–09 financial crisis, he insisted on working with retailers to bring them and his own company back to their pre-crisis profitability. A self-conscious bolstering of the Company's key constituencies, including the governing board, proved vital. "When we needed to undergo major restructuring," Freda recalls, "it wasn't an easy decision. But we had the Board's guidance, support, and trust at every stage."

Jon M. Huntsman, Jr., who served as Governor of Utah and US Ambassador to China and Singapore, had reached much the same view on the principle of personal fortitude. His administration in Utah had failed for several years to enact comprehensive tax reform he saw as vital for the state, he recalled, and failures of that magnitude can sometimes result more in "body counts" than in a reaffirmation of the original objectives.

But Huntsman insisted that his team press forward, accepting rather than deflecting blame for legislative setbacks, and repeatedly voicing his unequivocal support for the reform. Momentary failure is simply a price of progress, he says, a predictable product of taking significant risks inherent in making any major change. And from adversity, concludes Huntsman, you can learn important lessons, among them an abiding commitment to stand back up, however hard the knockdown: "We were more unified as a team each time we were able to reflect on our mistakes, dust ourselves off, and go at it again."

Strauss Zelnick, founder of media and communications private equity firm ZelnickMedia, has made a career of leading change in its most extreme form: the corporate turnaround. One principle he learned from living in that leadership chair is to pick your battles. Some companies cannot be turned around, he warns, "and if anyone thinks their executive skills are going to trump the facts, it's nonsense." His firm has been consistently able to work through its restructuring agendas, he reports, and he attributes much of that to careful selection: he would only work to resurrect companies that could indeed be transformed. By extension, the goals of change leadership are only as good as they are realistically achievable.

Edward D. Breen's change goals were as extreme as any leader has pursued—yet they remained attainable. After serving as the number two executive at Motorola, Breen took the leadership chair at Tyco International in 2002 at a moment when a management scandal had pushed Tyco to the edge of bankruptcy, a fate that had taken down both Enron and WorldCom for similar reasons at nearly the same time. To get through an enormous remake of a damaged company with more than 240,000 employees, Breen found that it was critical to think clearly and act decisively—despite the crisis and uncertainties of the moment—and then to provide unswerving support to his fresh team of lieutenants who would execute the remake.

William Clay Ford, Jr., Executive Chairman of Ford Motor Company, had faced a comparable challenge when auto sales went off a cliff during the financial crisis of 2008-09. Among the vital decisions that came from his leadership chair was the securing of a $26 billion credit line, the commitment to work closely with the company's unions, and a doubling down on research and development, all helping the automaker emerge from the financial crisis far stronger than did its domestic rivals.

Pressing for change but always keeping a clear eye on your North Star is also critical, urged Arthur O. Sulzberger, Jr., Chairman of The New York Times Company and Publisher of the *New York Times*. With the rise of digital media, his newspaper faced a set of wrenching decisions on how to charge for digital content. He knew he would have to creatively respond to the enormously disruptive power of the web and that he would have to do so quickly and flexibly. "If you establish a path in the world and say this is where we're heading and we've got to be there five years from now," he warns, "you'll be in trouble because the world is changing too fast."

Yet it is also important, Sulzberger emphasizes, to make those changes in ways that are aligned with the enterprise's ultimate purpose. "Our mission is to give all of you and the citizens of our world the kind of quality information you find necessary to make the decision to keep democracy alive," he explains, and for that he insisted that the company consistently focus on its enduring achievement whatever the momentary setbacks. William P. Lauder concurs: "No matter the type of company, as CEO, your job is to measure every decision against the company's mission, and keep your eye on the long-term vision."

TAKING THE LEADERSHIP CHAIR

An overarching theme emerges when listening to these executives tell their stories: the call for a holistic approach to decision making in the leadership chair. Taken together, these accounts demonstrate that there is no silver bullet—no single capability that transforms an ordinary individual into an outstanding leader. Thinking strategically, acting decisively, and communicating persuasively are certainly important characteristics of great leaders. So, too, are developing and inspiring; leveraging and preparing; and spearheading change.

> **"Leadership calls for a whole package, a simultaneous application of many capacities."**
>
> —MICHAEL USEEM, PH.D.

But from the inside accounts gathered in this volume, we are repeatedly reminded that leadership calls for a whole package, a simultaneous application of many capacities. And that is the great value William brings to this endeavor. By surveying so many diverse occupants of the leadership chair, he has developed a more complete, and thus more powerful, leadership template. It is a working model rooted in and road-tested by those who have served in the leadership chair, and it is a pragmatic model for those who aspire to hold a position that carries responsibility for others.

Not all of what those in these leadership chairs have done, however, should necessarily carry over. Like each of us, those featured in this volume face concerns and constraints unique to their perch. The reader's challenge is to selectively incorporate what can work and fit within their own leadership place. And that more personalized leadership model can be further refined and fleshed out by interviewing or informally talking with those who have led. Reading accounts about other leaders or by other leaders, such as Jim Collins' *Good to Great* and Sheryl Sandberg's *Lean In*, can prove invaluable as well.[2] Whatever the source of leadership ideas, and more are better than fewer, the accounts assembled here, along with those other resources can, together, furnish an essential foundation for successfully filling a leadership chair of one's own.

2   Jim Collins, *Good to Great: Why Some Companies Make the Leap . . . and Others Don't*, New York: HarperBusiness, 2001; Sheryl Sandberg, *Lean In: Women, Work, and the Will to Lead*, New York: Knopf, 2013.

AUTHOR'S NOTE

William P. Lauder

Not a day passes that I don't draw upon one of the many lessons I learned as a student at the Wharton School of the University of Pennsylvania.

At Wharton, I studied marketing and international business, which gave me a strong foundation for my career. One semester, simply to expand my horizons—and to explore a subject I found personally fascinating—I took a particularly eye-opening class about real estate with a professor named Bill Zucker.

On its face, Professor Zucker's class was fairly ordinary. Each week, we would meet for three hours and discuss real estate cases, approaching each assignment from a variety of angles.

But what made his class extraordinary was that instead of merely studying one case after another, we had the opportunity to discuss our readings and thinking with the real-life business leaders whose real-world challenges we were dissecting. Suddenly, we were hearing directly from these savvy, seasoned executives about how they navigated incredibly difficult issues.

While I never pursued a career in real estate, that semester has stayed with me—and that class' teachings have come in handy many times throughout my career. So when the Wharton School approached me with a request to design and lead a class for second-year MBA candidates, I knew exactly what I wanted to do.

Most top business schools—Wharton foremost among them—train students with an expectation that they will, upon graduation, be qualified and prepared to lead organizations, from start-ups to Fortune 500s. Academic rigor is par for the course, but there is a human element to corporate leadership that cannot be conveyed through even the best business books or case studies or spreadsheets. So in addition to providing an excellent academic education, the best schools should be intent on exposing their students to a practical perspective—the lessons one learns from actually serving in the C-suite.

In developing the course Decision Making in the Leadership Chair, my aspiration was to offer students a genuine firsthand look at crucial questions of leadership: Why and how do leaders make decisions? How do they successfully balance the interests of multiple stakeholders? How do they effectively navigate crises, manage organizational transitions, and weather uncertainty?

I wanted my students to gain a nuanced appreciation for the responsibilities that leaders have, both to their organizations and within their communities.

And thus, borrowing a page from Professor Zucker's playbook, I invited into my classroom accomplished executives—women and men who have led at the highest levels—to share their experiences and insights. I chose individuals with unique stories, who demonstrated their own distinct leadership styles, and who were challenged in different ways. As the course has progressed, these outstanding leaders have continued to share their teachings with each successive class of students.

In the pages that follow, I highlight a variety of outstanding examples of leadership. For example, in 2002, not long after Ed Breen left Motorola to take over the embattled US-based company Tyco, the papers were filled with news of its troubles. The previous CEO had been fired in disgrace, indicted and imprisoned on charges of misappropriating company funds; many other company officials soon met a similar fate. After years of cooking the books, Tyco was in dire financial straits. Breen, however, slowly but surely turned around the company, and today he's credited with bringing it back to life. As *USA Today* put it, "In 30 months, Breen . . . managed to turn one of the nation's most notorious and mistrusted companies into a respected member of the business establishment."[3]

I was, of course, well aware of Breen and his turnaround success long before inviting him to be a guest in my class. Like everyone else, I had read the papers.

But when Breen spoke with my Wharton students, what struck me most was a part of his story I'd not heard before: walking into Tyco, an organization barely on life support, he knew he had to fire the top three hundred executives. Right or wrong, they were tainted just by association. Breen knew he would lose the public's trust if he kept them in place. And yet, before he could ask them to leave, he needed to motivate them to continue working. He knew he could not clean up the mess without them—and they knew that he knew it, too.

As Breen shared with us his strategic, methodical approach to making the decisions that ultimately saved the company, he wasn't just lecturing—he was bringing us along in his thought process and giving us an inside look at the complexities of managing big decisions. It was a completely different profile in leadership than what most students study in business school.

Throughout the semester, we heard countless other stories just as illuminating.

After teaching this course for three years, I have been fortunate to witness its impact on my students. And what I have realized is that these valuable lessons are also deeply relevant to each of us at The Estée Lauder Companies—wherever we may sit.

Since our founding in 1946, The Estée Lauder Companies has been a learning organization, committed to developing our skills and evolving the way we do business in order to stay ahead of the changing world

---

3   Cauley, Leslie, "CEO Leads Troubled Tyco into Turnaround," *USA Today*, January 2005, http://usatoday.30.usatoday.com/money/industries/manufacturing/2005-01-23-tyco_x.htm.

around us. We are never satisfied with standing pat. We should never believe that we know everything.

This book was conceived in the spirit of the many educational opportunities available to employees of The Estée Lauder Companies: we want our people to continuously grow their knowledge and skills, because we know that our most important asset is our people. While we may not be able to bring every employee to Wharton, we see this as an opportunity to bring Wharton to you.

This is especially important because our Company asks and expects leadership from every chair. To continue promoting leadership, and to enable employees to better navigate the types of complex decisions we all face during our careers, we need to learn to think in multidimensional ways. My hope is that in reading this book, and in absorbing its lessons of real-life leadership, you will feel inspired to explore and develop your own leadership style. After all, in order to lead from every chair, we must learn from every chair.

ACKNOWLEDGMENTS

L ike nearly all journeys of learning and discovery, my class at the Wharton School of the University of Pennsylvania—Decision Making in the Leadership Chair—and the book it inspired was, and remains, a collaborative endeavor.

First and foremost, I am grateful to the Wharton School for affording me the opportunity to share a classroom with so many brilliant students for seven weeks each winter. Learning with—and learning from—the next generation of business leaders is an extraordinary experience.

Our class and the wisdom captured here would not have been possible without several members of the Wharton faculty, who were generous with their counsel and guidance at every stage of the process. Michael Useem, one of the world's leading academics on the topics of corporate leadership and governance, was my partner throughout, from conception to execution. He continues to be a sage adviser, and has shaped me into a better leader in front of the classroom and the boardroom alike.

Mauro Guillen, who wisely and ably heads the Lauder Institute at Wharton, is a trusted adviser and treasured friend. Adam Grant, Kathy Pearson, David Reibstein, David Wessels, Patti Williams, and Jerry Wind not only helped me to develop the curriculum, but also taught me how to become a better teacher. Each of these individuals continues to make invaluable contributions through our Company's many initiatives at the University of Pennsylvania.

Nick Lobuglio, my teaching assistant, worked tirelessly behind the scenes to manage, orchestrate, and facilitate. He will make an outstanding professor himself.

Our students and I were exceptionally privileged to host several of the most experienced and accomplished executives in the world: Edward D. Breen, Chairman of Tyco International; William Clay Ford, Jr.,

Executive Chairman of Ford Motor Company; Richard D. Parsons, former Chairman of AOL-Time Warner and Citigroup; James D. Robinson, IV, Co-Founder of the venture capital firm RRE Ventures; Arthur O. Sulzberger, Jr., Chairman and Publisher of the *New York Times*; Lauren Zalaznick, former Executive Vice President of NBC Universal; and our own President and Chief Executive Officer Fabrizio Freda. As leaders of, and advisers to, global businesses, they receive many invitations, and I thank them for sharing their inspiring stories and insights with our class and colleagues. They continue to be extraordinarily generous with their time, both in the classroom and in preparing this book with me.

I also owe an enormous debt of gratitude to the dozen leaders who allowed me to interview them—and from whom we hear in the pages that follow. I asked these visionary women and men to speak with me because, over the years, I have admired and learned from their inspiring successes. We all can take something from their fabulous stories and powerful advice.

For my part, I learn constantly from my tremendous colleagues at The Estée Lauder Companies. My trusted partner Fabrizio Freda brought a new level of "learner" leadership to The Estée Lauder Companies when he joined us as President and CEO. By developing our High-Touch Leadership Competencies Model—and placing it at the center of our organization's professional development process and performance development strategy—Fabrizio continues to empower our colleagues to optimize their leadership skills. I am endlessly amazed by his singular ability to inspire our team and equip our people with the tools they need to lead—and deliver—from every chair.

Every day, Phebe Farrow Port, SVP of Global Management Strategies and Chief of Staff to the President and CEO, translates our mission to be a learning organization into action. She is uniquely gifted as a developer of talent; she has a special gift for matching the right people with the right roles and for unlocking the capacities of others.

Dara Chamides, Global Executive Director of Executive Education, was (and is) my thought partner and collaborator on many of our initiatives for our most senior leaders. For many years, I thought about putting together a class like Decision Making in the Leadership Chair and a book like this. Dara was the one who brought both to life—and who made it an unforgettable, deeply enriching learning experience for our students, guests, and, especially, me.

Our strategic partners at West Wing Writers—Jonas Kieffer, Sarada Peri, and Jamie Serlin—have been indispensable collaborators. On every step of our *Decision Making in the Leadership Chair* adventure—from concept, to classroom, to company—they have been architects, ambassadors, and wordsmiths extraordinaire.

Finally, every page of this book bears the fingerprints of two very special people: my parents Evelyn and Leonard Lauder, who instilled the importance of education in their children and grandchildren. My mother taught us that no vision is beyond one's reach when we leave the borders of our comfort zones behind. My father taught us the importance of discipline, drive, and determination. With appreciation for all they taught me about these two hallmarks of leadership—imagining anew and pushing forward—this book is dedicated to them.

As is always the case, any errors are my own.

William P. Lauder
Fall 2015

THE ROLE OF THE CHIEF EXECUTIVE

LEADERSHIP SPOTLIGHT
Fabrizio Freda

A CONVERSATION WITH
Nancy Koehn, Ph.D.

THE ROLE OF THE CHIEF EXECUTIVE

The essence of great leadership is charting the right course for your organization while empowering your employees to steer the ship and raise the sails. As the pioneering scholar of leadership Warren Bennis put it, "Managers are people who do things right and leaders are people who do the right thing."

While technical business skills are essential, CEOs must also be adept in four key areas: inspiring employees to action; strategizing for stakeholders, not just shareholders; multiplying themselves and their expertise; and adapting to change.

Especially in large organizations with multiple businesses or brands, strong leaders must delegate not only responsibility, but also ownership and authority. To elicit the highest performance from employees, they need to foster a culture where each individual feels like the company's success is their own.

A favorite teaching of mine comes from the ancient Chinese philosopher Lao Tzu:

> A good leader is he whom people revere. An evil leader is he whom people despise. A great leader is he of whom people say, 'We did it ourselves.'

At the same time, in order to effectively lead, C-level executives need to do more than answer to a bottom line and the shareholders who watch it. They must first fully understand the ecosystem around them, including the motivations, needs, and interests of all stakeholders. For large companies, this can mean a diverse and disconnected collection of actors. But the extra effort of engaging stakeholders in decision making ultimately leads to greater value for all.

Great leaders are also not content to be islands of excellence. They are teachers, mentors, and counselors, and they multiply themselves and their expertise by training their employees to perform at their highest levels.

Finally, in a volatile world, leaders must be ready and able to adapt to change. They must remain flexible and keep their companies agile so they can thrive even in the face of uncertainty.

If this sounds like easy work, think again. As leadership expert and Harvard Business School historian Nancy Koehn says, it takes "courage, faith, commitment, and a strong sense of self."

It also takes great partnership.

That's why I am so grateful to have a brilliant and capable partner in Fabrizio Freda—my friend, colleague, and companion in leadership at The Estée Lauder Companies. During the last six years, as President and CEO, Fabrizio has helped me to chart our Company's strategic vision and take our business to new heights. It is only with the support of expert partners, trusted advisers, and talented, passionate employees at every level that leaders can balance their extraordinary responsibilities and deliver outstanding results.

> **"Managers are people who do things right and leaders are people who do the right thing."**
>
> —WARREN BENNIS

FABRIZIO FREDA

PARTNERS IN CHANGE

In 2008, four years into my tenure as CEO of The Estée Lauder Companies (ELC), I felt that sweeping change was just beyond the horizon. Consumers were becoming more connected and empowered. E-commerce was gaining momentum. Global demographics were shifting, including the rise of emerging markets and their middle classes. The business was performing well, but the beauty industry was evolving and our organization needed to adapt to ensure our continued success.

To face the change head-on and make the fundamental updates to the business structure that I felt were necessary, I realized I would need a partner who shared my vision and priorities. The moment I met Fabrizio Freda, I knew I had found that partner. Fabrizio is a brilliant strategist and results-oriented leader who had spent two decades in numerous leadership positions at Procter & Gamble before joining our Company as Chief Operating Officer. Later, when I became Executive Chairman, Fabrizio moved into the President and Chief Executive Officer role, forming what would become an extraordinary collaboration.

As CEO, Fabrizio has worked in concert with our Company's Executive Leadership Team to help accelerate many of the changes we initially identified as strategic imperatives. Together, amid a global financial crisis, we succeeded in refreshing the organization's strategy and structure and breaking down silos so that our Company could share ideas, best practices, and talent across our brands, while investing to support new capabilities. Unprecedented growth for the Company followed.

Behind our successes are a clear vision, a well-crafted strategy, and a unique collaborative partnership that has kept The Estée Lauder Companies one step ahead of change in the industry and our competition. Fabrizio has also been a partner in the classroom, joining my Wharton students during the winters of 2014 and 2015 to share insights and lessons from the first years of our partnership.

A CLEAR VISION

Our classroom presentation begins with The Estée Lauder Companies vision: *The global leader in prestige beauty: a well-diversified, brand-building powerhouse of unrivaled creativity and innovation.*

Defining this new vision for our Company's future was the first step Fabrizio and I took in our work together. This carefully crafted statement forms the foundation of ELC's effective strategy.

As Fabrizio explains, "Every single word here is a choice. And because it's a choice, it creates a direction for change. All of the changes we implemented started from the definition of this vision."

For example, the choice to become the "global leader in prestige beauty" meant that our Company would not dedicate time or resources to mass product development. The choice to be "well-diversified" drove our Company to make strategic investments in new and emerging markets, channels, and brands. The choice to be a "brand-building powerhouse" meant refocusing the brand portfolio on growing categories.

After the vision is defined, the second step is alignment. "Every leadership story requires alignment, because you cannot lead if you don't have followers," Fabrizio told my students in 2015. For Fabrizio and me, this meant engaging the Board, the Lauder family, and many key senior leaders from across the organization in a highly collaborative process. Many people were hesitant about change, but we worked to ensure that every voice was heard so that once the vision was agreed to, our organization could move forward in total alignment and with one voice.

REVERSE ENGINEERING

With our team aligned behind a shared vision, Fabrizio and I then began to reverse engineer against the vision to create the Company's strategy. "Strategy is about choices," Fabrizio explains. "It's about having a vision, looking at the alternative routes you can take to get there, and then choosing where to play and how to win."

While some companies approach the strategic process in terms of continuous improvement, under Fabrizio's leadership, our team focuses on reverse engineering.

The difference? As Fabrizio puts it, "Continuous improvement means starting from where you are today and, based on an analysis of your past experiences, taking the next steps forward toward your vision. Reverse engineering means you are considering what the world will look like ten years from now and determining, based on that, what has to come true eight years from now, six years from now, four years from now, and tomorrow morning, in order for your organization to succeed."

This is especially important in the fast-evolving beauty industry. "In a world where, five years from now, the business will be dramatically different from the past and present," Fabrizio told our students, "you have to decide where you want to be and then reverse engineer your success."

Reverse engineering often requires a fundamental shift in thinking, but it leads to the kind of forward-looking investments that are crucial to long-term value creation. As Fabrizio put it, "If you evolve your strategy on a continuous-improvement basis, how many companies are going to invest in the digital world in a disruptive way? How many companies are going to completely transform their distribution system? How many companies would have the persistence needed to win in emerging markets?"

Each of these initiatives has been central to the Company's long-term success, but organizations don't make these types of huge, strategic changes in a continuous-improvement model. They only make them based on vision—on a reverse-engineering model.

CRISIS AS A CATALYST

Reverse engineering can't predict the future or unplanned events, but it can guide you to an end goal. To advance the Company's strategic vision, Fabrizio and I had initially planned to gradually restructure the Company to speed up stagnant processes, strengthen alignment, and drive efficiencies.

But soon after Fabrizio's arrival in 2008, as we were planning to implement the first phase of the strategy, the financial crisis hit, upending the global economy. Fabrizio says it best: "Life starts when you stop planning." We had a clear and measured plan—only moderate changes over time—and then the ground shifted under our feet. "In retrospect, the lesson was clear," Fabrizio told my students. "Use a crisis to accelerate the changes you need to make because it helps people accept dramatic change."

Instead of evolving over several years, we decided to make all of the planned changes within just six months, because the risk associated with speed was dwarfed by the risk of inaction. These changes included redesigning brand clusters, creating a regional structure, designating enhanced multifunctional leadership teams, and clarifying processes, roles, and decision rights.

The crisis spurred momentum for this undertaking, and that momentum was perpetuated by Fabrizio's consistent message: change is a permanent thing.

Of course, implementing major changes takes buy-in from your leadership team, especially when change is accelerated. Once the Executive Leadership Team embraced the significant changes, and began leading those changes, they started to see exceptional results and gained even more confidence in the direction we had set out. And this affirmed another important lesson: change can only move at the speed of trust.

The Company's Board of Directors also played a critical role in helping us to navigate the financial crisis and adopt change ahead of the curve.

"When we needed to undergo major restructuring, it wasn't an easy decision," Fabrizio shared, "but we had the Board's guidance, support, and trust at every stage." Keeping in close communication with the Board throughout this challenging period allowed us to proceed with confidence.

ALLOCATING RESOURCES

The restructuring that took place as part of the accelerated strategic change yielded significant cost savings for our Company, which allowed us to allocate resources to build new capabilities. We added research and development platforms in Europe and Asia, brought consumer insights and new marketing capabilities in-house, and invested in new and emerging channels. Each of these investments represented a deliberate choice in support of the Company's strategy.

As Fabrizio often emphasizes, once choices are made about where to play and how to win, leaders must determine what capabilities are needed to execute the strategy and then allocate resources against those priorities.

This step is mission critical. As Fabrizio explained, "You might have strategic ideas, but if you don't have the resources or the capabilities in place to realize them, you don't have a strategy." And just as important as deciding where to invest is deciding where not to. For every area in which we chose to allocate resources, there were corresponding areas in which we determined not to invest.

In short, Fabrizio affirmed, four elements must be part of every strategic discussion: a clear vision; choices of where to play between the alternatives you have; choices of how to win in each of the areas where you have chosen to play; and a clear set of capabilities needed to achieve your goal. If any one of these four elements is missing, there are likely to be gaps in executing a strategy with excellence.

"My primary job as a leader," Fabrizio said, "is to help my team work through these elements and think more and more strategically every day."

A SOUND STRATEGY DRIVES PERFORMANCE

Since Fabrizio and I formed our partnership, the Company has taken fundamental steps to realize its vision. Today, The Estée Lauder Companies is the world leader in prestige beauty with a well-diversified brand portfolio and operations in a wide range of markets and channels. As Fabrizio reminds our colleagues, "Many companies write missions and vision statements and nothing happens. For us, it is happening. We are building our vision."

To help the Company continue delivering these strong results over the long term, Fabrizio enhanced the strategy process in 2012 by adding a new dimension—the Ten-Year Strategic Compass.

The Compass paints a picture of the industry across regions, channels, and categories ten years out. It helps the Company's leaders take into account long-term trends when setting the overall direction for the business.

"We know when we paint this picture that the numbers will not be precise," Fabrizio said, "but we are confident that the direction is right. That's why we call it a compass and not a map."

BRILLIANT PARTNERSHIPS, NOT HERO LEADERS

The last six years have been a time of considerable change for The Estée Lauder Companies. Our success during this period is a credit to the hard work and dedication of our employees and to the deeply collaborative partnership Fabrizio and I share. We counsel one another, exchange learnings, and alternate leading and following, depending on the situation.

> "Leadership isn't about leading at every moment, every second of the day . . . It's about knowing when to lead and when to follow. I have found that good leaders are also excellent followers in certain moments."
>
> —FABRIZIO FREDA

"Leadership isn't about leading at every moment, every second of the day," Fabrizio told my students. "It's about knowing when to lead and when to follow. I have found that good leaders are also excellent followers in certain moments."

And if there is one point on which we agree, it is this one: the era of the solitary, heroic CEO is over. "The future of leadership is in brilliant partnerships rather than lonely leaders," Fabrizio advises. "Trusted partners working together and exchanging ideas and input produce better results."

NANCY KOEHN, PH.D.

Nancy Koehn is a professor and historian at the Harvard Business School. She is the author of several books chronicling great entrepreneurs and leaders throughout history. Koehn is interested in how these individuals learned to lead effectively, including the impact they exercised and how they motivated and inspired those around them. She has studied, written, and spoken on how leadership lessons from the likes of Abraham Lincoln, Ernest Shackleton, and Rachel Carson can be applied to present-day challenges. Koehn is a frequent contributor to NPR, the *New York Times*, CNBC, CNN, and other news programs.

One of the leaders Koehn has studied in depth is Mrs. Estée Lauder, whose rise she chronicled in her 2001 book *Brand New: How Entrepreneurs Earned Consumers' Trust from Wedgwood to Dell*. In the book, Koehn recounts Mrs. Estée Lauder's keen entrepreneurial sense and deep insight into her customers' desires and motivations. Using these skills, Koehn explained, Mrs. Estée Lauder "constructed a meaningful identity for her products" that women to this day associate with quality and elegance.

Koehn shared insights from ELC's history and discussed the evolution of leadership from the days of US President Franklin Roosevelt to current Apple CEO Tim Cook. She explained how women in the boardroom are transforming corporate culture and how a new generation of millennial activists is wielding its power to effect change in business. Koehn's deep knowledge and historical perspective can help all of us understand our place in the long history of leadership, and how to use lessons from history's greatest leaders in our own daily lives.

asses, you often close with a great quote from the novelist David Foster Wallace: real leaders are people "who can help us overcome the limitations of our own individual laziness and selfishness and weakness and fear and get us to do better, harder things than we can get ourselves to do on our own." My question to you is, how do they do it? How do great leaders bring out the best in their employees and inspire them to push beyond their self-prescribed limits?

First, a leader starts with a worthy mission. They have to know where they are going and why it's a journey worth making. Whether we're talking about Mrs. Estée Lauder trying to build her cosmetic company and incite the early beauty advisers to sell new products in a new way, or Abraham Lincoln at the Gettysburg Address trying to get people to continue to invest in a war that was bloody beyond belief. The onus for articulating that mission over and over again, to every stakeholder, is on the leader.

Second, a leader puts the mission in context. They have to communicate not just what the mission means today, but why it matters in the context of the past and the future. Think about the Gettysburg Address. It's less than three hundred words, but it's one of the most brilliant and inspiring leadership speeches in the English language. It locates the mission in the present ("Now we are engaged in a great civil war"), reaches back into the past to explain its historical relevance ("Four score and seven years ago . . ."), and projects its impact into the future ("that government of the people, by the people, for the people, shall not perish from the earth").

> "If you can articulate those key pieces—a worthy mission, a larger context, and a role for each individual—you can inspire some truly amazing results."
>
> —NANCY KOEHN, PH.D.

Third, a leader helps individuals recognize their role in the mission. That's important because it's very hard for people to commit, to invest their time and energy, and to do something that scares them—even if it's something they believe in—if they don't understand their role in the larger cause. In a big organization, an executive may not be able to say to each person, "Here's what you're doing, and here's why it's critical for the mission," but they have to be able to, in a clear and succinct way, invest people personally in the broader purpose.

Mrs. Estée Lauder did this in her early work with beauty advisers, teaching them how to stand behind a counter and listen to consumers and close a sale. She made each of those women feel like they had a role in building the company and the brand by bringing beauty and the power of beauty to women.

If you can articulate those key pieces—a worthy mission, a larger context, and a role for each individual—you can inspire some truly amazing results.

Having studied generations of exceptional leaders, what do you see as the defining characteristics of the particularly great ones?

Courage, faith, commitment, and a strong sense of self. As a leader, you're going to experience periods where things are really hard. If you don't believe, at the most fundamental level, in what you're doing, then you're not going to be able to keep anyone else believing. The greatest leaders have all shared an unwavering commitment to their respective missions and used it to inspire others during difficult moments.

The ability to harness that inner strength, to perform regular gut checks, and to pivot when necessary—without losing sight of the goal— is essential to great leadership. And I'd say almost every great leader I've studied has had that ability to access those core muscles of courage, faith, and commitment in the face of obstacles.

Are certain leadership qualities timeless? In your estimation, would the great leaders of the nineteenth and early twentieth centuries still be effective today?

You'd have to be pretty adaptable and deft to make that jump. I think Mrs. Estée Lauder would probably do just fine. She was savvy, and she was a classic entrepreneur. The environment has changed in many ways, but there are certainly a few timeless principles when it comes to leadership that are just as important today as they were a century ago.

The first is the ability to manage the small but critical details of a business without losing sight of the larger picture—whether that's the state of oil refining in 1870 or what's happening in social media in 2014. For example, at ELC, a leader has to be able to weigh in on the specific details surrounding a new product launch, while also understanding that launch in the context of changing beauty paradigms and the exploding market for beauty products in, for instance, China.

The second timeless quality is the willingness and ability to put yourself in another person's shoes. Dale Carnegie wrote about this almost eighty years ago in *How to Win Friends and Influence People*, and it's still absolutely critical for leadership today. No matter who walks in the door of your office, or who's on the other side of the table, you have to be able to see things from their vantage point and use that empathy in service of your mission.

The third is the ability to commit wholly to the mission or the objective and, at the same time, demonstrate great dexterity and flexibility about the means to achieve it. That was as true for Mrs. Estée Lauder in 1950 as it is for the folks at the Gates Foundation today trying to figure out how to make a difference in the Ebola outbreak.

The fourth is effective and persistent communication. Lincoln didn't have the Internet, but he had a burgeoning and very prolific printing press and he used it every which way. The same is true of the best leaders today. They are relentless in articulating their vision. When you have an important message, you have to be willing to talk about it until you're blue in the face.

How have the demands of leadership changed over time?

We live in a world today in which every organization and every leader lives in a glass house. Transparency is no longer a choice an organization makes. News and information—true or not—travels at lightning speed. Leaders now have to be much more thoughtful and careful in the way they live their lives and communicate their messages. If you think that a manufacturing plant on the other side of the world isn't something that consumers or activists care about, think again. Everything is fair game.

Franklin Roosevelt didn't have to worry about this; he just winked and said to the press, "Please don't take pictures of me in my wheelchair or on my crutches," and they gamely acquiesced. Well, that world is gone. The backstory of a business, of an organization, of a political movement—even of one's personal life—is now part of the menu or the operating system or the software you're selling. For Tim Cook, the CEO of Apple, coming out as gay was significant not just from a personal standpoint, but from a business standpoint as well, because it communicated something to customers about the values of the company.

To that point, the era of the celebrity CEO seems to be waning now. Excellent leaders in the business world are no longer viewed as the all-knowing, all-seeing, all-powerful Oz of the past, but rather as very effective generals of very effective armies.

Absolutely. It's over. And with the end of that era comes some loss and some gain. One of the gains is that leaders are more focused today on communicating their own humanity. Tim Cook is kind of exhibit A, or Howard Schultz, who, as CEO, took responsibility for mistakes at Starbucks and was willing to say, "I don't have all the answers, but here's what I know."

There's a new focus on how leaders use their humanity to motivate people by appealing to our higher selves, which is the thing we're so thirsty for in leadership.

You mentioned the speed at which information travels today, and I'll add that the accessibility of information has increased significantly. How has that evolution created new challenges and opportunities for leaders?

It's interesting because there's been a centralization of certain kinds of power and authority in the last twenty-five years—around income, wealth, and privilege—and at the same time, there's been a great flattening of organizations in terms of consumer power.

Global activists using Twitter and the Internet can prompt an enormous amount of change in an organization by virtue of the information they disseminate. There's increasing attention being paid to the values of a company and the way it does business. That's only going to grow in strength.

All of that means that leaders have to be very attuned, not just to market research, not just to what the analysts are saying, not just to their shareholders, not even just to their customers—but to all of their stakeholders. There's now an entire world of connected people that are interested in the company, even if they're not yet on the other side of the counter.

The millennial generation sees their power as consumers and workers very differently than previous generations, and so for leaders, there's a new gauntlet that they have to pick up that isn't something Mrs. Estée Lauder, Marshall Field, or Henry Ford had to contend with when they were building their companies.

All of this is to say I don't think it's ever been, in some ways, more challenging to be an effective leader, and at the same time, more significant. With all these new gauntlets come new opportunities to change and shape the world and your organization's place in it.

As a historian, you know that women in the boardroom are still a relatively new phenomenon. My grandmother was a rare exception in her time. But today, women executives are more numerous than ever, and I'm proud they comprise half of our Board at The Estée Lauder Companies. From your vantage, how has the rise of women directors and executives changed corporate culture?

The rise of women directors and executives has unquestionably changed corporate culture. It has made it more open and revealed different ways of looking at the world. That's true of any group that comes into power that hasn't previously held it. They look at things differently than the traditional constituencies.

That's especially important in this flatter, more global, more diverse world. ELC's customers look much more varied than they did forty or even thirty years ago; its stakeholders are different, and the people holding its stock are different. So women in power, just like African American, Latino, and LGBT constituencies, help companies see the world in broader, more varied, and more integrated ways.

Do women leaders tend to approach decision making differently than their male counterparts?

In the wake of the financial crisis, there was some interesting research around whether, if there had been more women on Wall Street trading in mortgage-related securities, the outcome might have been different. That led to interesting findings about how women make decisions under pressure and otherwise.

Broadly construed, women tend to make more long-term bets than men. They tend to assess risk differently and more carefully. From an evolutionary perspective, that makes sense, because women have traditionally been responsible for managing the family and raising the children, a job that is all about long-term planning and decision making.

Companies need both—long-term planners and short-term risk takers—to succeed. So having both dimensions in the leadership chair is extremely valuable. I think women have brought that dimension to the table, and that's leading to better business decisions across the board.

What advice or wisdom do you have for young leaders in the first few chapters of their careers?

Recognize that you're going to have to make yourself into a great leader. It's not something that you're born with. You have to learn it. You're responsible for your own learning, so surround yourself with interesting people. Follow the cause or the mission that you love and believe in because that's going to make you a better student, and the better the student you are, the better the leader you'll become.

You should also recognize that you learn from every single experience—not just your successes and failures—but during all the days, months, and weeks in between. And you don't just learn in the arena where you want to exercise leadership. You learn from your friendships and from your dealings with the everyday transactions of life. You learn from your hobbies and from the people you work out with.

Everything is fair game to create the circumstances and the moments that will make you into a great leader, but you have to make the decision to get in the game. You have to choose the lifelong project of making yourself a better leader every single year.

MISSION

MISSION

Every single day, in a company the size of ours, there are millions of decisions being made. Of those millions, only a select few involve the direct input of the Executive Leadership Team. The simple fact is, leaders can't be personally involved in every decision at every level of a large company. There aren't enough hours in a day or days in the week—and even if there were, entrusting every decision to a small group of leaders is a recipe for inefficiency. So how do leaders keep a large and diverse company moving forward in unison?

By communicating and reinforcing a strong mission and a clear set of values that keep everyone on the team aligned.

Employees can only make good decisions when they're confident—and that confidence comes from a clear understanding of the vision and how it fits within the company mission. Organizations succeed when every member of the team feels ownership of the mission and understands the direction the company is headed.

Every company mission is unique, but successful missions share a few core qualities. They are rooted in the past and focused on the future. They are idealistic but realistic, ambitious but attainable, and comprehensive but unambiguous. Most importantly, they are universally embraced. If a mission feels forced, it's not going to be sustainable. The most powerful missions organize and inspire.

The job of a leader is to reinforce, enhance, challenge, and—when necessary—adapt the mission to changing circumstances. Arthur O. Sulzberger, Jr., Chairman of the New York Times Company, took on the latter task as the digital revolution upended the newspaper industry and challenged the *Times*' longstanding and deeply embedded mission.

For Alex Gorsky, Chairman and CEO of Johnson & Johnson, it was the opposite. Following a string of quality-control failures and amid lawsuits and federal investigations, Gorsky restored consumer and employee confidence by returning the company to the seventy-year-old values inscribed in its credo.

And as Governor of Utah, Jon M. Huntsman, Jr., encouraged his staff to keep the mission front and center by keeping it in their back pockets—literally. Huntsman, Jr., printed his administration's mission on laminated cards and asked his staff to carry them each day as a physical reminder of the work they were put in office to do.

As each of these stories demonstrates, leading a mission-driven organization can be a tricky task. But they also show another side. When the whole team is united and the goal is in sight, it's also the most rewarding.

ARTHUR O. SULZBERGER, JR.

FROM PRINTING TO CLICKING

When Adolph Ochs purchased the *New York Times* in 1896, it was a failing newspaper, the weakest of the then thirteen English-language newspapers in New York City. But under Ochs' leadership, the paper began to turn around, eventually expanding beyond its regional footprint to become one of the most read and respected newspapers in the world. Its instantly recognizable masthead carries the motto, "All the news that's fit to print."

Today, the *Times* is led by Arthur O. Sulzberger, Jr., Ochs' great-grandson. Sulzberger, who serves as Chairman of the New York Times Company and Publisher of the *New York Times*, has steered the nation's most lauded newspaper through the digital revolution, expanding its reach and thriving at a time when many other newspapers were collapsing. As the nature and economics of the newspaper industry has changed, the *Times* has changed with it, while remaining true to its unique and sacred mission.

A UNIQUE MISSION

The *New York Times*' core mission is to "enhance society by creating, collecting, and distributing high-quality news and information and opinion." Its responsibilities are to both the public good and its shareholders.

To better meet its responsibility to the public, the *Times* has developed a unique governing structure. Although the company is publicly owned, it issues dual-class stock, reserving the right to elect the majority of the board of directors for holders of the B shares. The vast majority of these B shares are held by the Sulzbergers in a family trust dedicated to the mission of maintaining the independence and integrity of the *New York Times* and its journalism.

"Because of the dual-class stock, we can focus on the long term," Sulzberger explained. The ability to maintain a long-term vision is an essential tool for the *Times* because it keeps the organization focused on the mission and "because it's giving us the freedom to make the investments necessary to adapt to a digital future."

But it's important that shareholders understand what they're getting into when they choose an investment with a unique structure and mission. As Sulzberger put it, "If you're coming in for short-term gain, there are a thousand better choices, but if you're coming in to see long-term growth, I believe we're going to be a great investment."

THE DIFFICULT QUESTION OF WIKILEAKS

Leading a mission-driven organization often involves difficult choices. The *New York Times* must constantly balance its responsibility to report the news with the highest standards of integrity with the significant implications its stories have on society. On more than one occasion, the decision to publish a controversial piece has come with grave consequences.

In 2011, for instance, the paper was approached by an organization called WikiLeaks. WikiLeaks had obtained a cache of illegally leaked military dispatches and diplomatic cables, including sensitive and classified information about the United States' wars in Iraq and Afghanistan. WikiLeaks offered the *Times*, along with two overseas newspapers, the first crack at reporting the findings.

Immediately, Sulzberger and the paper's senior editors faced many difficult questions: Could the information be trusted? Was it accurate? Could they legally and morally publish sensitive, illegally obtained materials that might jeopardize US national security and diplomatic relations?

Once the *Times* determined that, yes, the leaked information was reliable and accurate, Sulzberger and his colleagues felt a journalistic obligation to publish the information with supporting context and analysis.

"Our mission is to give the citizens of our world the kind of quality information they find necessary to make the decision to keep democracy alive," Sulzberger explained. "Because if they don't know what their governments are doing, then really, how do they know what lever to pull?"

Few companies have grappled with such perilous decisions. The *Times'* senior editors recognized that making public some of the information provided by WikiLeaks could potentially cost people their lives. This risk, Sulzberger underscored, is not one the newspaper takes lightly. "There are many things we know that we don't publish because we actually do believe it would do something damaging to the country or to individuals around the world," he said.

Yet, he also noted, "there is a cost, sometimes, to not publishing." If the *Times* were to ignore a story this big, the paper risked abrogating its responsibility to—and losing the trust of—its readers, as well as flouting its broader obligation to the public.

So the *Times* moved forward—slowly and carefully. That meant working with the White House and various federal agencies to redact any information that would put people's lives at risk or threaten national interests. "The amount of time we spent going through all of this was just stunning," Sulzberger recalled.

Of course, a decision like this requires more than time. Sulzberger's job was to methodically consider the implications of making one choice or another and to weigh that analysis against the *Times'* mission. He was conscious throughout that the common interest must outweigh the interests of the company. Sulzberger's challenge was to decide which option, publishing or not publishing, would better serve the public. Ultimately, that decision came down to careful, strategic thinking and smart judgment.

MISSION VS. ECONOMICS

Sometimes the stakeholder most damaged by the *Times'* decision to publish a story is the company itself. This was the case when it came to an investigation the *Times* published in October 2012 revealing that relatives of Chinese Prime Minister Wen Jiabao had accumulated billions in hidden wealth during his leadership. The Chinese government responded by swiftly blocking access to the *Times'* English-language and Chinese-language websites—cutting off access to more than a billion readers in the world's fastest growing economy, a major economic hit for the company. The website remains blocked today.

"That was the biggest financial-impact story I've ever had to deal with," Sulzberger said. "The minute we made the decision to publish that story, we knew we were going to be blocked in China for years." Other publications have held similar stories to preserve access to the Chinese market, Sulzberger said. "But for us it went to the core of our mission. There was no question that we were going to go forward with it."

The integrity of the *Times'* reporting has even greater financial implications in the digital age, Sulzberger explained. When Sulzberger joined the *Times,* the company's revenue was driven almost entirely by advertising. But today consumers are willing to pay more for quality content, and revenue is divided roughly 60-40 between consumer subscriptions and advertising, with the consumer segment continuing to grow.

"So more and more our responsibility financially isn't to the advertiser; it's to the consumer, the reader," Sulzberger said. "And if we don't meet the expectations of the reader, or if we're shown to have failed in their eyes, that's going to hurt us more in a financial sense than any other backlash we might face."

Does this philosophy hold even for stories that offend some of the *Times'* biggest advertisers? Sulzberger says yes. "At the end of the day, if we don't have the courage to publish the journalism that we think is valid, then our consumers won't come to us. And if our consumers don't come to us, our advertisers will have no one to reach anyway."

THE CHALLENGE FOR QUALITY JOURNALISM IN A DIGITAL WORLD

Effective leaders, however, must be careful not to conflate staying true to a mission with clinging to a static vision. Sulzberger observed that one of the biggest challenges organizations face is staying nimble in their thinking.

"We started building our digital presence roughly twenty years ago," Sulzberger said. "But as we all know, the nature of how people are coming to the web is changing. For example, it's much more social than we had ever imagined five years ago, and mobile has emerged as the preferred platform for the vast majority of our readers."

Adapting to these changes has meant integrating the newsroom and the business side of the organization in ways once foreign to the *Times,* and indeed, most traditional news outlets. "We've had to move to a culture in which the newsroom and the business side work collaboratively to create new product, including a range of app choices to drive readership," Sulzberger said. "That has been a significant cultural challenge."

The road to adaptation hasn't always been smooth. "We've had marketing failures. We've had design failures. But we've learned a lot," Sulzberger said. "And the most important lesson was how to collaborate and say to both sides, 'Get past this wall. The business side and the news side cannot operate as separate tranches.'"

Despite the challenges, Sulzberger is convinced change is the only way forward. "In order to take the next steps that are critical to our sustainability, we have to rethink the culture of the institution," Sulzberger said.

MISSION VS. CHANGE

Driving change can be especially difficult in a mission-driven organization like the *Times*. In the newsroom, journalists are laser-focused on producing the best journalism possible—with little patience reserved for other activities. So when Sulzberger's team began building the *Times'* digital presence and asking journalists to play an active role in promoting their stories on social media, they were met with more than a little resistance.

"The problem is change gets in the way of the mission," Sulzberger says. "It's so hard to change those cultures because the automatic response is to say, 'No, that's extraneous. That's a distraction. That's not part of my mission.'"

The real moment of change came many years ago, when the *Times* was in the early stage of building its digital presence. Tom Friedman, a *Times* columnist, met a reader on an international flight who had just read a column online that he had submitted only hours before.

"All of a sudden, Tom became the most powerful voice in the newsroom for online, because he understood that producing great journalism was only part of the mission. Getting that journalism into the hands of readers was equally important. And the Internet expanded our mission to incorporate both."

Today, every editor is responsible for both digital and print publication and every journalist is responsible for the production and the dissemination of their content via social media. This expanded mission has necessitated other changes within the newsroom.

"If we're asking more of our journalists, we have to make sure they are empowered to deliver on those responsibilities." One of the biggest barriers remains the speed of decision making. "In some cases, we're still operating at print speed when we need to be moving at digital speed."

No matter the industry, Sulzberger said, in times of change, organizations need leaders who are prepared to take chances. "If you don't have a leader who's prepared to be aggressive in this time of change, you're not going to get to where you need to be," Sulzberger said. "We're in a place now where we have to test, learn, and fail. If we're not failing, we're not trying hard enough."

GOVERNOR JON M. HUNTSMAN, JR.

Jon M. Huntsman, Jr., is a former two-term Governor of Utah, former Ambassador to China and Singapore, and distinguished business executive serving on the boards of Ford Motor Company, Chevron, Caterpillar, and numerous other institutions. He's known for his pragmatic approach to leadership and his ability to work with members of both political parties, traits that made him a natural choice for his current role as Co-Chairman of No Labels, a bipartisan organization dedicated to cutting through the perpetual gridlock in the United States Congress.

Huntsman's career has mirrored his philosophy. The Republican governor of a Republican-leaning state left office in 2009 to serve as Democratic President Barack Obama's Ambassador to China. Huntsman spoke about his experiences in both of these roles and shared how the challenges he faced and lessons he learned have shaped his conception of leadership.

When a mining disaster shook Utah in the midst of his governorship, Huntsman learned the importance of leading with heart and putting people first. When he transitioned to the role of ambassador, he learned that the most effective leaders must also know how to follow. Throughout his career, he's witnessed how something as simple as an open door can unite a team and change the culture of an office. These lessons and more can serve all of us as we lead from every chair at ELC.

Tell me about your decision to run for governor. What prompted it?

It was really my family—my daughters, specifically—that convinced me that we needed to run. Utah at the time was in the midst of an economic downturn, and we were losing our most important asset, the next generation of educated young people, to surrounding states where the economies and opportunities were better.

I knew Utah, and I knew it had a lot to offer. I thought that with the right leadership and ideas, we could get the state moving in the right direction again. So as a family, we decided to go for it.

You'd never run for office before. How did you know where to begin? How did you build your platform and get others on board with your candidacy?

We were new to politics, so we didn't have an extensive network of people to draw from for campaign strategy and management. A lot of it just had to come from our instincts, which turned out to be the best thing in the world.

We got into the race with pure intentions. We wanted to improve the economic prospects for our state. Throughout the campaign, my focus was squarely on the things I believed in my heart of hearts I could do for the people of Utah. If other noncore issues came up during the campaign, I'd say, "You're going to have to go talk to other candidates. I don't do that. What I can promise is that I will bring new ideas and leadership to the table and lift our economy by improving our competitiveness and the job situation."

There was no pandering and no gimmicks, and that authenticity drew people to our campaign.

Tell me about your first days in office. How did you reorient your leadership style from campaign mode to management mode?

It's pretty surreal. The election is held, and you wake up the next morning and look at yourself in the mirror and say, "Now what?" I've been out there campaigning for a year talking about what I think I can do to help the people of Utah, and now I've got to make it a reality.

The first thing I did was find people who could staff a new administration. Often, you get people elected to political office, and they come in and operate like politicians. They make decisions along partisan lines, they hire on partisan lines, and they don't veer from the partisan message that's been broadcast by party headquarters.

That was never my approach. I wasn't elected as a politician. I was elected to lead. And I was elected very specifically to help revitalize the economic prospects of the state. To do that, I needed the best people around me, no matter what their political affiliation.

So I went out to leaders within our community—in business, in education, in public safety—and I told them I didn't care what party they belonged to; I didn't even care if they had voted for me. I needed them to come join my administration and help me make a difference for the state.

So you've got your team in place. How do you establish the kind of culture you need to be successful?

During the first week or two I sat down with my cabinet and laid out the principles I wanted to define my administration.

The first was trust. We were there to serve one constituency, and that was the public. We were custodians of the public trust, and I knew that the minute we lost public trust, we would be goners.

The second principle was transparency. I never had a day when I closed my office door. Executives close their doors, and those working around them assume something backhanded is going on. It's just human nature. The only way forward is to open the doors and open the culture so everyone feels they have a fair shot. If you've got a grievance, you can come in. If you've got a great idea, you can come in. You're never locked out.

You spoke about your economic platform, how committed you were to making real progress on those issues. How did you keep everyone else focused on the initial goals you set out to accomplish?

It's definitely a challenge. It's easy in a large bureaucracy for people to venture off onto tangents that maybe were important in earlier years, or that individuals think are important at that time but aren't central to the collective mission.

> **"It's easy . . . to venture off onto tangents that aren't . . . central to the collective mission."**
>
> —JON M. HUNTSMAN, JR.

During those first few weeks, I sat with my cabinet and mapped out how we were going to accomplish each of the objectives we laid out in our campaign. Then I had laminated cards made with those priorities listed on them.

Everyone on my staff—including me—carried those cards around in our pockets every day until we had checked off all of our goals. It was a simple, effective tool that kept everyone motivated and focused on the task at hand. We also invited some sharp management consultants to work with us in developing metrics for progress.

You had plenty of success as governor, but what about the times when you couldn't accomplish the goal, when you suffered a setback or ultimately failed to achieve the intended outcome? As a leader, how did you approach those disappointments and help your team overcome them?

The typical political thing to do is to engage in the body count. If something goes wrong, if something fails, you find somebody to fire and you move on with the next thing.

I never wanted to operate that way, and as the leader, I let my team know that ultimately, I was the responsible party. They were around the table as members of my cabinet because I had enough faith and trust in them to put them there. We weren't going to be perfect, but I wasn't going to let them down, and I trusted they wouldn't let me down.

We failed the first two years to pass our plan for comprehensive tax reform. Ultimately we got it done, but part of moving forward each time was reminding my team that failure is part of the process. It's not the end point. It's just a step in the process. And it's actually a good thing because from failure and adversity you can learn some important lessons. We were more unified as a team each time we were able to reflect on our mistakes, dust ourselves off, and go at it again. All ten economic-development priorities were ultimately accomplished.

Tell us about a time your leadership skills were put to the test. What did the experience teach you, and how have those lessons served you since?

Two years into my first term as governor we had a major mining disaster that put our state on the front pages of every newspaper and on television, 24/7, throughout the world.

A group of miners had been trapped underground in the collapse. We found out later they had all died instantly, but for about two to three weeks we didn't know if there were survivors. Federal rescue teams came in, the international media descended as rapidly as they could get into town, and these two little mining towns, of no more than a few thousand each, were suddenly thrust into the international spotlight as they waited to hear if their loved ones were alive. It was incredibly emotional. People were angry, they were scared, and they wanted answers.

There's no manual for how to manage a crisis like that. It's just completely up to your instincts and trusting the judgment of the people you've got around you.

My first instinct was to go and meet with the family members. We showed up at a local elementary school, and I spent hours and hours each day with the families, crying on shoulders, bringing them the latest news, much of which was not good.

All the cameras from around the world were outside waiting for family members to walk out and break down publicly or to complain or blame somebody for the disaster. And through it all, I came to the conclusion that the leadership part was pretty simple: you put people first, and you make sure they know you are with them, and that you are doing everything you possibly can in an open, honest way.

The second critically important piece was speaking to the media. People needed to hear what was happening from the chief executive of the state, and the families needed someone to speak on their behalf and say we are not going to give up.

Of course, it didn't end well. But it ended with the communities feeling as though we had done our very, very best.

In 2009, you left the governor's office to become Ambassador to China. You went from managing the state of Utah to managing one of the most complex international relationships in the world. You had a lot of disparate interests clamoring for your attention and a lot of moving pieces that make up the US mission there. How did you get everyone moving in the same direction?

Just as I had done with the laminated pocket cards, I started by setting the agenda. I knew if we set out to accomplish 150 things, we were going to end up accomplishing nothing. So we identified a few key priorities—a manageable number of things that we could get done that represented the most important US interests in China—and we started building a strategy and interagency coordination around them.

Each time I visited Washington, I'd meet with leaders in the administration and Congress, and I'd be able to say, "Here's what we're doing in China and why it's important to the overall strategy."

How did you build a rapport with your team where they trusted your vision but also felt confident bringing their own ideas to the table?

I made it a point to get out of my office, which is something ambassadors rarely do. In the beginning, when I wanted to talk to senior embassy staff, I went and sat in their offices. We'd sit and talk for an hour at a time, but mostly I was listening and learning.

That was the key to building a collaborative environment where we could have meetings and everyone could exhale and be themselves. I wasn't unknown to them. They didn't have to put on pretenses. We had developed a personal rapport, which led to a stronger professional relationship.

They knew I had an open-door policy, which didn't exist before, and a lot of the information was filtered through a set of special assistants, and then refined further, and then put on the ambassador's desk.

I knew it wasn't a traditional management structure, but I wanted every one of them to know they had access to me. They could walk through the door, and they didn't have to go through what had been a stifling bureaucratic process. In most cases, they never took advantage of it, but always knew I would see them if needed.

> "I sat with my cabinet and mapped out how we were going to accomplish each of the objectives we laid out in our campaign. Then I had laminated cards made with those priorities listed on them. Everyone on my staff—including me—carried those cards around in our pockets every day until we had checked off all of our goals."
>
> —JON M. HUNTSMAN, JR.

It strikes me that in some of your posts, you had great responsibility with limited authority; in others, you had great authority with limited responsibility; and, as governor, you had a unique amalgam of responsibility and authority. How do you get stuff done in each kind of leadership role?

I think the most important thing is to understand the parameters of your authority going into different roles and the importance of knowing when to lead and when to follow.

As governor of the state, you have the state constitution that guides you and you've got a legislature with whom you've got to work to get anything done. But the authority is singularly yours. You create a budget every year, you define your priorities, and then you go to work fighting for them.

As an ambassador, it's a completely different ball game. On one hand, you're a singular leader within the country to which you're posted. In China, there are two thousand men and women in the American embassy and five consulates looking to you to set the direction. On the other hand, you're just one participant of many in the interagency policy process that includes the Secretary of Defense, Secretary of State, President, and others. You're in there arguing in favor of a particular direction, but in the end, it's the President's decision.

So going from governor to ambassador as I did, you have to be able to subordinate your ego and understand that it's important sometimes to be a follower, too. It draws from both sides of your head and certainly consumes every management skill or trick you've ever learned going from one to the other.

If you could share one piece of advice or a kernel of wisdom with young aspiring leaders in the first few chapters of their careers, what would it be?

To lead with your heart. A lot of people lead with their head, which is good, and that should be part of the equation as well. But not enough people lead with their heart, which is to say, there's an emotional-intelligence component to the best examples in leadership.

You've got to be smart. You've got to know the issues. You've got to have all the technical stuff down. But in cases like a mining disaster, it's just as important to be able to lead with your heart.

Leading with your heart gains you loyalty, it brings in new constituencies, and it allows you to solidify relationships with your team that will serve you throughout your career.

ALEX GORSKY

Alex Gorsky is the Chairman and CEO of Johnson & Johnson, the global health care giant. He started there in 1988 as a pharmaceutical sales representative and climbed the ranks from J&J's pharmaceutical business in Europe, the Middle East, and Africa to the company's surgical-care and medical device divisions.

A West Point graduate, Gorsky is known for his decisive and disciplined approach to leadership. He assumed the role of CEO in 2012, as the company was facing crises related to a string of product recalls. Over the next two years, Gorsky and his leadership team led a turnaround that put J&J back on top with growing profits and rigorous quality-control standards.

Gorsky spoke about the tough decisions he made during those early days and the important role Johnson & Johnson's credo played in restoring employee and consumer confidence. He shared lessons from his days as an army lieutenant ("how to listen and lead with humility") as well as his early years at Johnson & Johnson ("Never underestimate the impact you can have with two minutes of your time"). These lessons can inspire all of us as we collaborate to take on challenges at ELC.

During your tenure at J&J, you have repeatedly cited the company's seventy-year-old credo as J&J's "moral compass." How does the credo influence decision making at J&J?

Our credo is a set of values that guides our decisions on a daily basis. It was written by General Robert Wood Johnson, who was the son of one of our founders and a pretty progressive thinker in his time.

General Johnson believed that businesses had to earn the right to participate in society, and on the eve of the company going public, he wrote the credo to ensure the company would not lose its soul.

From that day forward, it's been a critical part of our identity as a company. It's literally etched in the walls at our New Jersey headquarters, but more than that, it's part of every conversation and decision we make here.

We look at every situation and ask, "What does this mean for patients and doctors, for our employees and our communities, and ultimately for our shareholders?" We know we haven't lived up to our standards if we don't satisfy all those constituencies. There's always going to be a certain degree of trade-off, but in the end, we aren't going to do something if it's going to compromise the fundamental commitment we have to each of them.

How do you make the credo relevant to everyone at J&J? How do you ensure that it's more than a set of aspirational values—and that the company is fulfilling its promises, not just to shareholders, but also to stakeholders, on a day-to-day basis?

About eighteen months ago we asked every employee in the organization to get into groups and talk about what the credo meant to them.

We called it the "Credo Challenge," and the idea was to bring the credo to life for every employee. It was an opportunity for everyone to take a step back and answer the question, "How does this apply to my job?"

We also gave them real scenarios to work through where, frankly, we hadn't lived up to our credo values, and in each one, we asked them to think about how they would handle it differently.

This was something we did at every level, including with the members of our board. And I think they all would tell you it was one of the

JOHNSON: OUR CREDO

We believe our first responsibility is to the doctors, nurses, and patients, to mothers and fathers and all others who use our products and services. In meeting their needs everything we do must be of high quality. We must constantly strive to reduce our costs in order to maintain reasonable prices. Customers' orders must be serviced promptly and accurately. Our suppliers and distributors must have an opportunity to make a fair profit.

We are responsible to our employees, the men and women who work with us throughout the world. Everyone must be considered as an individual. We must respect their dignity and recognize their merit. They must have a sense of security in their jobs. Compensation must be fair and adequate, and working conditions clean, orderly, and safe. We must be mindful of ways to help our employees fulfill their family obligations. Employees must feel free to make suggestions and complaints. There must be equal opportunity for employment, development, and advancement for those qualified. We must provide competent management, and their actions must be just and ethical.

We are responsible to the communities in which we live and work and to the world community as well. We must be good citizens, support good works and charities, and pay our fair share of taxes. We must encourage civic improvements and better health and education. We must maintain in good order the property we are privileged to use, protecting the environment and natural resources.

Our final responsibility is to our stockholders. Business must make a sound profit. We must experiment with new ideas. Research must be carried on, innovative programs developed, and mistakes paid for. New equipment must be purchased, new facilities provided, and new products launched. Reserves must be created to provide for adverse times. When we operate according to these principles, the stockholders should realize a fair return.

most meaningful and seminal experiences they've had as a board member, of any board they've served on.

Once you have everyone on the same page in terms of the values, how do you hold your employees accountable for them?

Every two years we ask all of our employees to complete a "Credo Survey." It's an online questionnaire about every aspect of our business, from the range of customers that we reach with our products, to how we treat our suppliers, to our innovation, and the list goes on. In each of these categories, the questions relate directly back to our credo. So for our employees we might ask, "Are you getting adequate feedback? Do you have access to career-development services?" If not, then we know we have more work to do.

The results help us evaluate our progress from the enterprise level all the way down to the team level. Ultimately, they became part of the review process for our leaders. Our leaders, in turn, know they are going to be held accountable for their performance in every category, and they pay close attention to those metrics as a result.

You're a West Point graduate, and you spent six years in the US Army before entering the corporate world. How has your military background influenced you as a leader?

I think one of the greatest lessons I learned in the military was how to listen and how to lead with humility.

The structure of the Army is such that a new West Point graduate holds a higher rank than an enlisted soldier who's served for years. It's a tricky dynamic, and if you come in thinking you're ready to start handing out orders, you're in for a rude awakening.

I'll never forget being a brand new lieutenant and walking into my first meeting with my platoon sergeant, who was a thirty-five-year-old high-school-educated veteran. He stood up and saluted me and then said, "Sir, sit on down and let me tell you the way we do things around here."

It was a humbling experience, and it also taught me an incredible lesson about the difference between uneducated and unintelligent. The soldiers I worked with may not have had the privilege of going to the great schools I attended, but they were wicked smart, and they could connect the dots very quickly.

Later in my career, I learned that the opposite is also true. Just because you have a lot of initials behind your name doesn't necessarily make you smart or effective. There are many different qualities that make up an effective leader, and education is just one factor. That's a lesson I've taken into every one of my jobs going forward.

You've held a number of positions during your twenty-six years at Johnson & Johnson, starting on the ground floor as a sales rep and rising through the company's ranks to become chairman and CEO. In other words, before you became a leader, you worked with—and for—a number of them. How have their leadership styles influenced yours?

Earlier in my career at J&J, the president of one of our companies was a mentor of mine. I remember going to him right after I had been named as his successor and asking him for advice. His advice to me was, "Alex, don't ever underestimate the impact you can have with two minutes of your time."

He asked me, "Do you remember the first time you met me?" and I said, "Well, of course." I was a representative in a training program at the time, and I never forgot that the president of the company had stopped and said hello to me, that he knew me by name, and he had remembered that we both happened to be from Kansas City.

And he said, "Well, I'm sorry to tell you, but I don't remember that. But that's my whole point. By taking a minute to connect—something that for you may be a relatively minor task—you can engage and have a lasting impact on someone."

I think about that all the time, and in my role today I'm always asking myself, how can I use a minute to connect with people at all levels in our organization and inspire them in the same way?

Have there been any negative examples that have shaped you as a leader? Moments where you looked at someone who was managing you and said, "I will never do that when I'm in that position."

I have been very fortunate throughout my career to work for some great leaders who mentored and coached me along the way. I have also had a few negative experiences that also taught me a lot about leadership.

In one of my previous roles as a general manager, I had a number of situations that made it crucial to have frequent and open communication with my manager. The executive that was in charge of my division didn't put in the effort to check in on a regular basis and build up the confidence, trust, and fundamental rapport that we needed to carry on our day-to-day business.

I bear part of that responsibility, of course, but the experience taught me that consistent communication is critical to good leadership. It doesn't have to be a formal one-hour sit-down; sometimes just a three-minute check-in can make all the difference.

It's a lot like a bank account. If you make consistent deposits over time, in the end you have a great deal of wealth to draw upon. If you don't, and then you try to make a big deposit right before you want to withdraw, you won't have the same level of interest.

You mentioned trust as a key component of leadership and as one of the things you bank over time. How do you build trust as a leader so that those you lead trust your vision, and you, in turn, trust them to execute that vision?

I think there are two important pieces. The first is fairly simplistic: do what you say you're going to do. And it goes both ways. What I commit to my employees, I have to deliver, and I expect the same in return.

The second piece is transparency. I've always valued leaders who are open to collaboration and who bring others into the decision-making process. It's much easier to sign on to someone else's vision when you've had a chance to offer input and had a role in the process.

You took the reins at J&J during a challenging time when quality-control problems, lawsuits, and FDA investigations were threatening consumer confidence and company profits. Today, J&J is back on top with growing sales, an expanding global footprint, and a thriving innovation pipeline. What did it take to steer the company through this difficult period? Were there any trade-offs or tough choices that you had to make?

We have about 260 companies around the world, so that means even if every one of them has a good day every day of the year except one, I can still have a bad day every day. Part of this job is that there are a lot of crises du jour.

Coming in, the first step I took was to reaffirm our commitment to the credo. I talked about it during every meeting and worked to make it relevant for all of our employees. It was important to me from the start to unite people around a common set of values and expectations for our work going forward.

The second major step was to create a clear and explicit set of corporate priorities. Johnson & Johnson is a large and complex organization that for many years had been run in a very decentralized manner. That approach was great for spurring growth and innovation, but it had also potentially led to problems in quality control.

At the end of the day, you can't run a $75 billion corporation the same way you would run a $10 billion corporation, especially in a changing market environment. So I laid out a list of three priorities that were must-dos for our company—and I made it clear to our employees, our shareholders, and our board that these were things we were going to accomplish above all else.

That gave the organization a clear sense of direction, and each time we delivered on one of our priorities, we regained confidence in our ability to set targets and meet them.

You're in an industry that is all about the next innovation—the next disruption—that moves treatment and knowledge ahead. How do you foster that culture of innovation in your company?

I think you've got to live it, breathe it, and drive for it in everything you do. And for us, the biggest source of inspiration is our desire to help people live longer, healthier, and happier lives. The only way we can deliver on that aspiration is innovation.

In the world of science, in particular, the model for innovation has evolved significantly in recent years. If you went back just ten or fifteen years ago, much of our science was done inside our own discovery labs. Today, with the Internet and the pace at which information travels, science is much more ubiquitous. So a critical component of our thinking about innovation today is making sure we're connected with thought leaders, academic centers, and entrepreneurs in communities around the world where some of the best knowledge and insights are originating.

If you could share one piece of advice, one kernel of wisdom, to young, aspiring leaders in the first chapters of their careers, what would it be?

My advice is to take care of yourself and your health. In today's environment, the pace, the pressure, the challenges, and all the travel involved in leading a company can take a significant toll on you as an individual. And in the end, who we are as an individual is who we are as a leader. The healthier and more energetic you are as a person, the better you will be at your job.

Coming from someone who leads the world's largest health care company, I can tell you that the best kind of health care is well care—which is to say, taking care of yourself. When you think about building good habits for business, the habits you build now around making time to reenergize and managing work-life balance are just as important as any strategy statement or project-management approach.

BIG SWINGS

LEADERSHIP SPOTLIGHT
Edward D. Breen

A CONVERSATION WITH
Sarah Robb O'Hagan

A CONVERSATION WITH
Mellody Hobson

BIG SWINGS

I n the course of a career, a leader makes thousands of decisions and remembers very few. But for every leader, there are a few decisions that will always stand out, which—like it or not—can never be forgotten. These few are the "big swings"—the risks that change the trajectory of a company and industry.

The big swings are big for a reason: the value of their success is extraordinary, but the price of their failure can be equally devastating. So it should come as no surprise that big swings often encounter big resistance, and not just from inside the company.

When I first proposed opening freestanding stores for our Origins brand, I faced major resistance from one of our core customers: department stores. Going forward with the plan meant risking one of our most important relationships, but I was confident it was the right move for our business and for the brand. Ultimately, my instincts turned out to be correct, and our big swing with Origins heralded a major shift in the industry.

Sometimes leaders take big swings to capitalize on a promising or innovative idea. Other times they are forced into action by a looming crisis. Ed Breen, former CEO and current Chairman of Tyco International, has taken both in his career, and—to use his words—his "batting average is pretty high." For example, with Tyco embroiled in controversy, Breen convinced the company's entire board to step down, an unorthodox move that ultimately saved Tyco's reputation and helped the company emerge from the crisis stronger than before.

Mellody Hobson, President of Ariel Investments, has spent her career monitoring and evaluating the big swings as she advises investors on the most promising companies. But the 2008 financial crisis presented the biggest swing of her career, as she led her team through the delicate work of rebuilding the company after the crash.

And for Sarah Robb O'Hagan, President of Equinox and former Global President of Gatorade, the bold move to reinvent an outmoded but closely guarded brand design led to a resurgence of Gatorade as the top choice for serious athletes.

Big swings happen in every industry, and it's up to leaders to trust their instincts, step up to the plate, and—with a little bit of luck—hit it out of the park.

EDWARD D. BREEN

LEADING THROUGH A RESTRUCTURING

The afternoon of July 25, 2002 was a memorable one for Edward D. Breen and Tyco International. First, CNBC reported a rumor that the beleaguered company was preparing to file for bankruptcy. A few hours later, with its stock in a virtual free fall, Tyco announced Breen as its new CEO.

From these inauspicious beginnings came a decade of unprecedented success for Tyco under the leadership of Breen, who continues to serve as Tyco's chairman. Handed the reins of a company plagued by scandal and perilously close to bankruptcy, Breen took bold steps to secure his shareholders' trust and restore his employees' faith in their company. As a result of his actions, Tyco not only evaded bankruptcy, but the company also returned to profitability and regained its reputation for integrity.

THE FOUR FLOORS OF BUSINESS LEADERSHIP

Building a business is like building a house. If you want to build something that can stand the test of time, Breen explained, you need a solid foundation. For a business, that foundation is made up of its values. Tyco's four main values are integrity, excellence, teamwork, and accountability. The CEO is responsible for integrating these values into all levels of the company's culture and ensuring that they influence every action taken or decision made by any board member or employee.

Above the foundation is the first floor, where the work is done and where a company finds its operational rhythm. According to Breen, it takes both a strong offense and a strong defense to achieve a successful operational rhythm. In business leadership, offense is about investing in new areas, and defense is about minimizing internal waste. Correctly balancing these sends a strong message: "We need to stop wasting money because we're going to put it into growing this company."

As the company begins generating cash, it's time to build the second floor. The second floor is where decisions are made about cash allocation, which is crucially important to driving shareholder value. Spend money wisely, and your company will continue to grow. But spend it foolishly, and you'll end up falling behind competitors that are smarter money managers.

And finally, the business' roof is made up of the big swings—that is, the big ideas with the potential to fundamentally and permanently move the stock price of a company. Big swings aren't just little gambles—they're the big risks, like splitting a company up or making a conglomerate-sized purchase. "At the end of the day, the report card on the CEO is long-term shareholder value that's sustained," Breen explained. "And I always keep that in mind when we're thinking about a big swing."

Each of these floors of leadership builds upon the others. You can't make big swings without cash. You won't have cash without a smart operating rhythm. And nothing matters if you don't have a solid bedrock of values.

LESSONS FROM A CRISIS

As Tyco experienced, without that foundation of solid values, a house is liable to collapse.

When Breen arrived at the company in 2002, it was embroiled in a major corporate scandal that left few of its top executives untouched. The Manhattan District Attorney's office had already indicted former CEO Dennis Kozlowski for massive tax fraud and placed many others, including Tyco's CFO, under investigation. Meanwhile, the SEC was poring over the company's accounting practices and uncovering troubling irregularities.

Friends, colleagues, and reporters were all asking Breen the same question: Why would you go to Tyco when it's getting ready to go bankrupt and the rats are coming out?

But Breen was up for the challenge: "I get bored just running a company. I like the turnaround aspect of it."

He'd come to the right place.

By 1:00 p.m. on his first day, Breen found himself in a meeting with several of Tyco's largest investors, all of whom were panicked about a possible bankruptcy. "I had about thirty percent of our investor base sitting in a meeting with me. And I've been at the company since about seven in the morning. This is how crazy it got."

Given the extreme circumstances, Breen had to prioritize his time and focus on only the most immediate issues, the first of which was avoiding bankruptcy.

Breen started by defining Tyco's constituencies and triaging their needs. They fell into eight groups: (1) creditors and bondholders, (2) customers, (3) employees, (4) shareholders, (5) suppliers, (6) the board of directors, (7) government regulators, and (8) the local community.

As is true for any company, each of Tyco's constituencies had its own concerns and needs, and Breen, as CEO, was responsible for addressing all of them—from suppliers at risk of going under to employees who were ashamed to be seen in the community wearing their Tyco T-shirts.

At different moments during a company's lifetime, various constituencies take different levels of priority and require different things from the CEO. For instance, Breen explained, in the midst of crisis, government regulators demanded the most immediate attention because of their power over Tyco's ability to raise money.

"All stakeholders are important, because any one of them can take the company down," Breen said. "But when I've got a fire burning around me, I have to prioritize the regulators. Because if I can't get the issues resolved with the regulators, if I can't get over the bankruptcy issue, it won't matter if the employees are happy or not. I'm never going to get to that point."

Breen also had to find a way to make a substantial break from the past in order to reestablish Tyco's integrity and credibility. That's why one of his first acts as CEO was to fire the very board of directors that hired him. "In this case, it was very clear in my mind that the board had to go," he recalled.

It was an unprecedented move in the history of the company, but Breen was convinced that in order to save Tyco, the company needed to cut ties with its past image and tainted leadership. It was also the right move for the board members—though they may not have all agreed at the time—to leave before their reputations were sullied by their association with the old Tyco.

But in this difficult time, it wasn't enough for Breen to take the necessary actions—he had to make sure that others knew that he was doing everything necessary to turn Tyco around. "In a crisis, you have to communicate, communicate, communicate all the time and be very honest," Breen emphasized. Otherwise, the only side of the story that stakeholders will get is what they read in the paper.

THE "NONTRADITIONAL SKILL SET": MANAGING AND LEVERAGING PEOPLE

For all of their differences, these constituencies shared one thing in common: a human element. This, Breen emphasized, is the area where CEOs must shine. A CEO's success, he explained, is largely dependent on his or her ability to appeal to people. This "psychologist role"

demands a nontraditional skill set that is nonetheless essential to effective leadership.

This is especially important at a company that suffered such a
severe reputational blow. Faced with endless press coverage of corrup-
tion at the top, a parade of indictments, and looming bankruptcy, it
was easy for the public to forget the many real people—and many good
people—who made up Tyco.

When Breen reminded investigators that Tyco had 240,000 employees with families—essentially a million people—whose lives were rid-
ing on the outcome of the investigation, he was able to minimize the
tension, and the hostility, and have a more productive conversation.
"You've got to work with us," Breen urged the regulators.

Breen demonstrated these very same leadership skills when he
brought on titans like Jack Krol, former Chairman and CEO of the
DuPont Company, and the late Jerome York, former President and
CEO of Harwinton Capital, to help reassure stakeholders that Tyco was
back on the right path. On the day he announced Jerry York's hiring,
the market responded immediately. It was equally important for Breen
to leverage his people skills to implement the hardest decisions. Convincing Tyco's board to resign en masse required delicate communication and a deft touch.

Finally, in high-stress situations, effective leaders must also manage not only their own stress, but also that of their team. In times of
crisis, it's crucial for a CEO to give his or her team the tools and support they need to stay calm, think clearly, and make the right decisions
under pressure.

PASSION, INTEGRITY, AND MOVING THE NEEDLE

Breen is fond of a quote by Henry David Thoreau: "Most men live lives
of quiet desperation." To avoid such a fate, he advised young people to

follow their passions. Happiness is more likely when you do what you love rather than pursuing money or job titles.

While passion is important, integrity is, too. After seeing firsthand how devastating the loss of it can be, Breen recognizes that a leader's job is to guard their integrity at all times—and never to give it up. "You can't control everything that happens to you in life, but you can control what you do with your integrity," Breen said. "It's yours, and nobody can take it from you."

And it's important for leaders to set strict priorities not only in times of crisis, but at all times. At the top of the list should be a relentless commitment to "moving the needle." Otherwise, companies get stuck. And it's up to great leaders to ensure that, in good times as well as in crisis, they are leading a forward charge.

SARAH ROBB O'HAGAN

Sarah Robb O'Hagan is president of global luxury fitness company Equinox, which is made up of the Equinox, SoulCycle, Blink Fitness, and Pure Yoga brands. Before joining Equinox, Robb O'Hagan served as Global President of Gatorade, where she led the brand's transformation from sports-drink company to sports-performance-fueling company and the launch of its successful G Series line of products. She has also held senior marketing and management roles at Nike, Virgin, and other companies.

A lifelong fitness enthusiast, Robb O'Hagan has used her passion for health and wellness to fuel her success in business. With sales slipping at Gatorade, Robb O'Hagan developed and implemented a bold strategy to diversify the company's offerings and restore its reputation as a leading innovator in sports nutrition. Her success earned her a spot on *Forbes'* list of the most powerful women in sports and *Fast Company's* list of the most creative people in business.

Robb O'Hagan described her penchant for taking workout meetings at Equinox clubs and her quest to transform her own fitness regime. She spoke about standing up to skeptics, and the important role her past failures played in building her courage as a leader. Her advice on embracing innovation ("Remember what you're in business to do") and overcoming obstacles ("Make failure your fuel") can help inspire the bold, visionary leaders in all of us.

As the President of Equinox, you're facing a fitness industry that's gone high-tech, and consumers who are wholeheartedly embracing

that change. Hot new wearable gadgets are flying off the shelves. How are you adapting your company to integrate this new wave of fitness technology? How do you push your team to think ahead to Equinox 2.0?

Have you been in my meetings? Equinox 2.0 is exactly what we're calling it. Everyone's been disrupted by technology in recent years, but the fitness industry in particular has been ground zero for a massive amount of disruptive innovation. A lot more people, particularly in Silicon Valley, are clamoring to get into the health and wellness industry because health has become the new wealth. The money the luxury consumer might have spent on a Chanel bag a few years ago is now more likely to be spent on fitness classes at SoulCycle.

So it's an industry that's attracting a lot of attention and investment, and at first that kind of rapid innovation can be overwhelming. I remember feeling panicked a few years ago wondering if we were already behind the eight ball because we hadn't come out with our own fitness tracker. That's when you have to take a step back and remember what you're in business to do. We're not in the tracking business. We're in the business of interpreting information and using it to coach human beings. Our innovation strategy needed to be not "Let's chase this," but rather "Let's lead this. Let's use this as a complementary addition to the landscape that's going to help our business be better."

What does the new Equinox 2.0 look like?

We've spent the last couple of years investing pretty heavily in a platform that's going to enable us to aggregate all the data coming in, whether you're tracking with an app or a wearable device like the Apple Watch. And then we're putting it all into one platform and, more importantly, saying, "Okay, what can we do with this data against your specific health goals to help us coach you more effectively?"

That was the big aha moment for us, when we realized we could use technology to take the membership experience that had always been one to two hours a day and make it what I call an "always-on partner-ship." Wherever you are, you can take our app and any other device you use and share information with your trainer. Then he or she can tailor your workout to your specific needs.

Equinox is a self-described "temple of well-being." How do you walk the walk and foster this same culture for yourself and for your employees in their own lives?

Luckily for me, I work in a field I am genuinely passionate about. Fitness and sports have always been a huge part of my life, so walking the walk has been very easy here.

Since I started at Equinox, I've gone out of my way not only to work out in the clubs so I can spend time there with the teams, but to take my business meetings at the gym as well.

The first time I met Bobbi Brown, who is a great member of the ELC family, I said to her, "Well, we can have lunch, or we can work out together." So a whole group from her team came, and we all did a group fitness class together. It was great. I do workout meetings all the time.

When you're a leader, you have to be aware that everyone is always observing your behavior. If I'm not showing my passion for the business and the offering, how can I expect the rest of the team to?

Has working at Equinox changed your personal-fitness regime?

Absolutely. One of the things I did when I first came to Equinox was to turn myself into a personal experiment. I went to our personal training team and said, "Okay, tell me everything that we believe in philosophically around movement, nutrition, and sleep," and then I put it into practice. So for example, I was one of those classic five-hour-a-night sleepers; I'm now an eight-hour-a-night sleeper. It has transformed my life.

It was great personally, but it was also important for me to do as a leader. First, because, quite frankly, if this is what our team is recommending for our members, who am I if I don't try it? And second, because when I'm in a public forum now and we're talking about trends in health and fitness, I can speak to our sleep recommendations from personal experience, as opposed to just reading it out of a textbook.

Part of your life's work has been working to increase the access of girls in underserved communities to sports. What inspired you to get involved in this effort?

I played a lot of sports growing up, and there's actually a direct connection between girls playing sports and future leadership potential. According to one recent study, 80 percent of Fortune 500 female executives say that they played sports in high school. And girls who play sports in high school are 40 percent more likely to get a college degree. So there are well-known benefits to being involved in sports from a young age, especially if you're coming from a challenging home environment.

Yet, particularly in this country, girls drop out of sports at twice the rate of boys by the age of fourteen. So when a boy comes home and says to his dad, "I don't want to play sports anymore," his dad says, "That's unacceptable." When a girl does, her parents are more likely to say, "Ok."

The work I've done with the US State Department Council to Empower Women and Girls Through Sport and the Women's Sports Foundation is about giving young women the resources and encouragement to stay in the game so that we can stop them from walking away from their potential as leaders.

Going back in time, when you first began your career at Gatorade, sales were going nowhere fast. As I understand it, you took some big risks with the marketing budget to turn it around and at one point

**pitched an idea to your boss that would re-spin the brand entirely.
How did you know it was the right call?**

My first assessment was that we needed a transformational brand
strategy. The logo, everything was just so tired. I knew we needed to be
bold to turn things around. So three months into my tenure there, we
made the shift from Gatorade to "G."

> **"We needed a
> transformational
> brand strategy."**
>
> —SARAH ROBB O'HAGAN

It was probably a naïve decision, to be
honest with you. This was a brand that
had gone largely unchanged for more
than three decades, and now people are
suddenly saying, "I can't find Gatorade.
It looks different."

Then, just after we changed over to this new logo, the recession
hit and the entire bottom fell out of the business. I was on maternity
leave at the time, and I'm getting panicked calls from my bosses asking
me what the hell is going on. But it was interesting because all of the
retailers and everybody were up in arms, and I'm sitting at home with
my baby on the couch watching social media and seeing that kids are
actually catching on to this thing super quickly. You could just see there
was something there. And I just knew in my gut, we have got to hold on
to this, because we've created something and it means something to
them. So then we had to figure out how to drive it through.

How did you win over the skeptics?

There were so many skeptics, but I had two big things on my side.
One was that the business had been declining anyway, so we needed to
do something. We could have gone back to the old approach. But that
wasn't working. The only path was forward.

The other thing was, I was really the only person in the room at the
top executive level with a background in sports. I knew the consumer,
and I trusted my judgment. So I stuck to my guns. We built a very strong

team to execute our strategy, and within the next year we launched the G Series. From there, things turned around very quickly.

The biggest lesson, besides trusting your instincts, is that you have to stay true to what the brand is about. Gatorade had been relying on a lot of "rented" nonathletic consumers for sales before the recession, and then when the recession hit, those consumers disappeared. We needed to cater to our core: the athletes who were going to stay with us because we're the leaders in innovative sports nutrition. If you invest in your core, you're going to get results.

How do you think about recruiting and cultivating talent at Equinox? What do you look for in the people you hire?

I am a really big believer in diversity—and not only in the classic sense, but also in diversity of industry experiences. At Equinox, we like to say we never look at the competition; instead we look at the outside industry experiences our members are getting exposed to. I'm going to get a lot more insight from high-end hotels, retailers, and airlines than I am from the standard fitness industry.

> "We could have gone back to the old approach. But that wasn't working. The only path was forward."
>
> —SARAH ROBB O'HAGAN

That also applies to how we think about talent at the corporate level. We've brought in a lot of people from very different backgrounds. Our CMO came from Starwood Hotels, and we've got people from fashion and from sports. When you blend those experiences, it's pretty amazing the kind of original thought that comes together.

In terms of developing talent, I think you have to inspire employees at every level to see a career path beyond where they currently are. So many of our people who start out as trainers and membership advisers have gone on to amazing careers in the corporate office. Part of our job is to help our employees see how their talents can be—pardon the pun—exercised in ways beyond the job they may be doing today.

Aside from industry experience, are there certain characteristics or personality types that you look for?

I tend to look around the edges. I want to make sure you've got all the qualifications, but I'm also looking for that fire in the belly, that passion and that person who's going to stick themselves out and push you, and therefore the business, a little bit further than someone else. But I do think you have to balance it. When you're building a team, you can't have everybody be that same profile. So you've got to figure out how everyone's going to fit together with each other and look for different characteristics.

How do you deal with somebody who expects that the next stop is your job? Someone who comes in and expects between years two and four that they're going to be tapped as CEO?

I've certainly seen that phenomenon of young people coming out of school either expecting to be CEO in four years or to be Mark Zuckerberg in four years. Or having this notion of, "I'm just going to build a start-up, sell it, be worth a bazillion dollars, and I'm done." And I want to say to them, "It's really the journey that's so much more important."

I mean, I am actually one of those people, who at many steps in my career was young for my role. People would say, "How are you running a global five-billion-dollar business and you're thirty-nine?" And to be honest with you, there were a few steps where I got ahead of myself. There are moments in my career where I knew—you just have that feeling as a leader of, "Oh God, I wish I'd had a little bit more time here or there or wherever." Just to develop the skills or my confidence a little more.

And that's one thing I wish I could tell my younger self. By the time you've got gray hair, you're probably feeling pretty confident because you've got those experiences in your back pocket. It's scary when you don't.

If you could share one piece of advice, one kernel of wisdom to young leaders in the first few chapters of their careers, what would it be?

To make failure your fuel. I think when you're young—I was certainly like this—you're ambitious and you have this kind of upward linear progression pattern in your mind. You think every step has to be up and up and up.

In actuality, looking back, it was really the epic failures that were the most pivotal. I've been laid off; I've gotten fired before; I've had all the really bad experiences career-wise that would make most people just go, "Ugh, it's all over." And at the time, I did think it was all over.

But those are the same experiences that enabled me, when I was at Gatorade, to stand up for something that no one else agreed with and say, "It's okay, because if I get fired, I'll survive. I've survived before."

Those two things—failure and courage—go hand in hand.

MELLODY HOBSON

Mellody Hobson is President of Ariel Investments, a Chicago-based investment firm, and serves as Chairman of the Board for Dream-Works Animation SKG. She also serves on the Board of Directors for The Estée Lauder Companies and Starbucks Corporation and in leadership roles at a number of community and education-oriented nonprofits.

A twenty-three-year veteran of the finance industry, Hobson began her career as an intern at Ariel and climbed the ranks to become president in just a decade. Today, she is a leading advocate for financial literacy and investor education and a regular contributor to CBS news programs, providing insights on economic trends, finance, and the markets.

Hobson shared the secret behind her meteoric rise at Ariel and the leadership lessons she's learned throughout her career. She explained her strategy for managing the 2008 financial crisis ("Go to really smart people and ask for help") and for getting the best out of each member of her team ("They don't all have to be Michael Jordan"). Her hard-won insights and thoughtful lessons can help all of us weather storms and deliver on our full potential.

The story behind your career at Ariel Investments is amazing. You started at Ariel as an intern in college and rose to become the firm's president in only ten years. To what do you attribute your success?

I was always conditioned to work really hard. It was in my DNA, and I think that's really important, especially when you work in an entrepreneurial endeavor, or in a small firm where everyone has to wear a lot of hats. I have a lot of stamina and still do. I can basically outwork most people. It's something that's a bit of a badge of honor for me, and I think that really gave me a leg up.

What did you learn along the way to make you a more effective leader?

I learned that everyone couldn't work like me, and I had to learn to get the best out of people. My business partner, John Rogers, taught me that lesson. We were working together on the night before Thanksgiving, and we were the only two people in the office. I looked at him and said, "How can this be? How are we the only two people here?" We had real things to get done. And he said, "That's why you're in charge."

I just couldn't understand it. So he said, "Mellody, think of it this way. The Chicago Bulls basketball team has won multiple national championships. Phil Jackson, their head coach, can look for basketball players all over the world, but there's only one Michael Jordan. Scottie Pippen blocks, and Dennis Rodman rebounds, and Steve Kerr sinks three-point shots. Every player has a role, and when they are focused on being the best in that role, the team wins. But they don't all have to be Michael Jordan." And it just suddenly clicked for me: you get what you need out of people. They don't all have to be the greatest ever; they just have to make their contribution so that the whole is greater than any individual part.

How has that lesson influenced how you lead today? How do you understand the strengths of the people on your team and then get them to focus their energy on those strengths?

There was a great coach at Ariel that helped me put that lesson into practice. He said to me, "Mellody, you're already successful. Now your job is to make everyone else successful. If you make them successful, the firm will be successful."

So to extend the basketball metaphor, as the head coach at Ariel, my job is to help my players succeed. Sometimes that means realigning my expectations with the reality of who a person is versus who I think they should be. The best thing you can possibly do for an individual is to let them be who they are. That doesn't mean you settle, and that's the fine line that I've always struggled with. You still have to push—the challenge is to figure out where and how hard to push to get the best result.

You're known as an advocate for patient investing. In fact, if I recall correctly, the Ariel logo is a turtle. And you've described patience as an important element of Ariel's business strategy. What does that mean to you, and what's the importance of patience in business, and for leaders in general?

Patience has been instrumental in my success. I've had one job since I graduated from college. I've been at Ariel for twenty-three years. They say in my graduating class of 1,100 people, I'm the only person who's had the same work phone number since I graduated.

I think the fact that I saw myself working at Ariel for my entire career was something that helped me a lot. I was not a person who was looking and thinking the grass was greener on the other side of the fence. I wasn't looking for that next job opportunity, which meant I could stay very focused on my work.

So I don't think it's an accident that I work in a firm that has a turtle as a logo. I think, if anything, our world has gotten so short term in its thinking that it is actually making us less successful as a society and as individuals in a company.

Now, patience doesn't mean a lack of urgency, because I have a sense of urgency about everything I do. But at the same time, I'm always thinking about what something could be over decades rather than just in the immediate term.

Have you ever found your patience being tested?

Many times. Our team would probably tell you that I'm very impatient in a lot of areas. I take a long-term view, but you've still got to make things happen on a day-to-day basis. Sometimes those things are small, and sometimes they're big. But something should be happening every day.

So as an example, when we go to see clients or prospects, I have rules around thank-you notes—how fast they have to be out, how fast notes that we take on our meetings have to be in our system, so that if something happened to me or someone else, you could pick up the relationship seamlessly. And I don't want to see a situation where it's three weeks later and the notes still aren't there. So I've asked my teammates to agree that a letter is out within seven days and notes are in the system within ten days.

How do you enforce the deadlines after you set them?

My colleagues had a hard time meeting the thank-you-note deadlines at first. I'd remind them, and it would get better for a little while, and then it would fall off again. So finally I walked into our meeting one day and said to my team, "Here's what's going to happen: every time you miss the deadline it's five hundred dollars." And that was it—problem solved. From that point on, no one ever missed.

I didn't want it to get to that point, and I had people from the team who were very upset that it did, but ultimately it was the only thing that worked.

Have you used this tool on anything else?

I've only used that tool for thank-you notes, and only because other, less heavy-handed attempts had already failed. You can't overplay your hand. Everything is not urgent.

Have you discovered any other effective tools for getting your team motivated to do the right thing without your day-to-day pushing?

I don't think you can ever stop pushing. I think that is the nature of leadership. And that doesn't mean I don't have very talented, driven people around me. I do. But there is a certain energy that is necessary to win. You see it with team captains and with quarterbacks. That energy is essential, and it can't ever dissipate, or you'll find yourself less successful. So even though I have a great team doing great work, I can't ever ease up. And one day it won't be my energy; it'll be someone else's driving the team forward.

Let's change subjects for a moment. You're a strong advocate for diversity, especially diversity in leadership roles. We're seeing progressive change at the top of companies and government, but from your vantage point, what has to change in order for more companies to embrace and insist on diversity in their leadership?

I don't think we're seeing enough change, and unfortunately, in a lot of ways, I think we've moved backwards. There are five African American leaders of Fortune 500 companies today. There is just one woman among them.[4] I look at those statistics and think, how is it that we aren't further along?

I've been to many, many corporate events where I have been the only black person—where I've been asked if I was with the band or been asked to get someone a drink. That tells you a lot about a society.

I think if you want to make real progress, there has to be a commitment. You have to force the issue; you can't just talk about it. I'm not talking about quotas. I'm talking about policies like the Rooney Rule in the National Football League, where if you have an open coaching

---

4　Gregory Wallace, "Only 5 Black CEOs at 500 Biggest Companies," *CNN Money*, January 29, 2015, http://money.cnn.com/2015/01/29/news/economy/mcdonalds-ceo-diversity/.

position, you have to interview minority candidates. If you have criteria that say at a senior level in any given company, the slate has to be diverse for open positions, you're going to find yourself selecting people that you didn't expect to select.

But it's one of these things that takes a real commitment. The companies that have been most effective at it are the ones who understand why it is in their best interest—why they will have more customers because of it, why they will be more successful because of inclusion.

Ariel is a company with a diverse leadership team. How has that diversity fueled your success?

One thing that distinguishes Ariel is that inside our firm we have very different points of view. And that makes for better investment because you don't get groupthink. Scott Page wrote a book called *The Difference* that all of us read. He said if you're around the table and you're arguing with your colleagues, it's a very good thing. You should be afraid when you are all unanimous in agreement. We absolutely believe that to be true. It's a harder way to live and manage, but it actually leads to a better outcome.

The same is true at ELC. I know I bring different energy to your Board than Paul Fribourg and Barry Sternlicht. I know that Wei Sun Christianson brings different energy than I bring and different ideas and different experiences. And I think that makes us better. If most companies had that throughout their organizations, they would be even better.

You led Ariel Investments through the financial crisis in 2008—a challenging time for every business, but particularly for investment firms. What did it take to steer the company through this difficult period? What tough choices did you face, and how did you handle them?

We had the toughest year in the history of our firm in 2008. In terms of our investment performance, our flagship fund was down 48 percent, when we had always outperformed in a down market. It felt like we were not delivering on the Ariel promise, which is a big deal to a client.

Then we had to do the first layoff in the history of our firm, and that was very, very hard. We laid off nineteen people. It was on the news that night. I was devastated because I felt like I'd let them down. I knew I didn't have all the answers, so the best thing I did during that period was to go to really smart people and ask them for help.

What was the best advice you received?

I talked to George Roche, the former CEO of global investment firm T. Rowe Price, before the layoffs, and he told me, "The worst thing you could possibly do is be stingy. It's going to sound counterintuitive, but give these people anything and everything they need—if you do right by them in a very hard time, everyone will benefit in the long run."

> **"In a blizzard, you never look up at the storm. You only watch your feet. You only try to get from one place to another."**
>
> —MELLODY HOBSON

I called former US Senator Bill Bradley, who served with me on the board of directors at Starbucks, the day I had to do the layoffs. I was very nervous, and he said, "Mellody, whatever you do, don't cry." He said, "This is not about you. It's about them, and your tears will not make them feel better." That was hard to do, but he was absolutely right.

I talked to my husband on a particularly horrible day for the markets, and he said to me, "Mellody, you grew up in Chicago. What do you know about getting through a blizzard?" And I said, "I don't know." And he said, "In a blizzard, you never look up at the storm. You only watch your feet. You only try to get from one place to another. Do not look up at the storm, Mellody. Just watch your feet." That was such great advice. And I went to work that day and said to my team, we're not going to look up at the madness. For the research and investment team, they are going to deal stock by stock. For the client service and the marketing team, client by client, letter by letter. We aren't going to try to sum all of this up and take all of this on because it was too vague and too hard to do. And just like that, step by step, we rebuilt ourselves.

In light of everything we've discussed and all your experience, if you could share one piece of advice, one kernel of wisdom for young leaders in the first stage of their careers, what would it be?

Be patient, and don't ever settle.

INNOVATION

INNOVATION

At The Estée Lauder Companies, creativity is one of our greatest assets. It's how we continue to push the envelope and capture our consumers' imaginations year after year, and why we coined the phrase "creativity driven, consumer inspired" to describe our approach to product and brand development.

Of course, innovation and creativity come in many different forms and apply to more than just products and ideas. There is creativity in management and in the way we work with people. There is creativity in experiences and the way we chart our careers. There is creativity in how we balance the demands of work and manage our personal lives.

To fully unleash a great team's potential, leaders must foster a culture of creativity—in all its forms—by encouraging their employees to challenge the status quo, take risks, try new things, and not be afraid to fail in the process.

This is the approach that led former NBCUniversal executive Lauren Zalaznick to reinvent the floundering Bravo network and subsequently transform the entire landscape of cable television. It's been a touchstone throughout her career in media as she has moved from movies, to television, to journalism, technology, and venture capital.

It's the same approach that helped Dr. Judith Rodin, President of the Rockefeller Foundation, infuse a century-old institution with new energy—and a renewed focus on innovation and resilience.

And it's the vision at the heart of the Huntsman Corporation, founded by Jon Huntsman, Sr., which cycled through hundreds of failed product ideas before landing on the innovation that would launch it to stratospheric success.

In business as in life, there can be no reward without a measure of risk. Helping their teams identify risks worth taking; ensuring they have the support they need to innovate, test, and learn; and granting them permission to try and fail is the ultimate job of every creative leader.

LAUREN ZALAZNICK

AN UNLIKELY EXECUTIVE

Lauren Zalaznick has devoted her career in media to transforming the cultural landscape. From her start as an independent feature film producer to her role as a transformational television executive and media visionary, Zalaznick is widely regarded as the face of—and a driving force for—creativity and innovation in her industry.

Zalaznick freely admits that she is an unlikely executive. In fact, she thinks the caption under her high school yearbook photo should have said as much: "Least likely corporate executive on the face of the earth. Ever."

But sometimes it takes an unlikely exec to accomplish an extraordinary feat. And Zalaznick has delivered feat after feat throughout her career—nowhere more so than in her tenure over ten years at NBC Universal. Zalaznick transformed Bravo, one of the cable networks she oversaw, from the thirty-first most watched channel to the eighth, capturing a uniquely upscale audience and pioneering such cultural sensations as *Project Runway, Top Chef,* and the *Real Housewives* franchise. Today, she sits on the boards of companies like Shazam and Penguin Random House and serves as an adviser to media company Refinery29, venture capital firm Greycroft Partners, and other creative enterprises. She's also launched a must-read weekly newsletter, the aptly named *LZ Sunday Paper,* a compilation of the week's top stories about, and frequently by, women in business.

DEBUNKING THE MYTH OF DISRUPTION

Like the deployment of the skill itself, defining the term *creativity* is difficult, though its value for business has never been in doubt. Technical skills come in and out of vogue, but demand for individuals with creative instincts has never waned.

Today, however, creativity is often represented by a new euphemism: disruption. And that, Zalaznick cautioned, "is a very dangerous thing."

In our start-up age of rapid technological advancement, *disruption* has become the ultimate in business buzzwords, associated with wildly successful companies from Twitter to Uber. But while disruption can mean a ticket to unimaginable success, it can be equally destructive to business, Zalaznick said.

"Disruption has taken on this mythical quality in business today," Zalaznick said. "But the truth is, disruption is a risky enterprise. In fact, the precursor to the term *disruptor* was *risk taker*." Disruption, she emphasized, "is not necessarily creative nor is it always the right way to grow a business. Disruptive ideas that don't work out destroy businesses, and disruptive ideas that aren't executed well never turn into businesses at all."

Many of the most disruptive businesses end up losing money, Zalaznick explained, because the idea behind them took shape ahead of the business model. "The biggest disruptors are often young start-ups that have nothing to lose," Zalaznick said. "Old, established companies, on the other hand, have everything to lose." How do you reconcile those two things and keep an established company innovative? "To me, that's true creativity in leadership," Zalaznick said.

Innovation can come in all forms: in product, in process, even in the management of a company. And it doesn't have to be exciting to be impactful. "There are plenty of cool companies that aren't particularly innovative and many boring, uncool companies that have generated unbelievable innovation and creativity," Zalaznick said.

ANTICIPATING THE ZEITGEIST

During Zalaznick's tenure as an executive vice president at NBCU, she saw firsthand the value of anticipating the next big thing and the consequences that come with clinging to the status quo.

At the time, the television industry found itself disrupted by the emergence of a new innovation: on-demand television. "We saw it coming," Zalaznick said, "but we did not, as a company and as an industry, react well to the DVR threat."

At the time, NBCU's leadership was debating the launch of Hulu, a website that allowed viewers to stream the network's shows on demand. Many people were hesitant about going digital, worrying that online streaming would devalue the network's content. And at first, Zalaznick said, that's exactly what happened.

"It was the right idea, if an imperfect one," Zalaznick said. "Hulu was a place where at least we could benefit from the audience who watched our programs online. But elsewhere in the digital realm, viewers escaped traditional measurement metrics and, thus, our fair share of advertising revenue."

Adapting to this model meant completely changing the rules of the advertising upfront to take into account online viewers. "We did it in two phases, both bad," Zalaznick admitted. Ultimately, the network found a formula that worked, and it has since been successful. But in dragging its feet, Zalaznick said, the network missed an opportunity to get ahead of the trend.

"As great as the Hulu innovation was, it lagged behind the real marketplace concern rather than leading it," Zalaznick said. "In Hulu, we were able to create another place where we could capture viewers. But we completely underestimated the total transformation of how viewers were going to watch—via subscription video on demand and, in particular, on mobile platforms."

Recognizing these shifts is critical to leading innovation. To find good examples, one need look no further than the growing segment of companies capitalizing on the sharing economy. In the case of the sharing economy, Zalaznick said, entrepreneurs sensed a shift in the balance of power that tipped the scales away from traditional companies and in favor of the empowered consumer. "When you look at our sharing economy today—companies like Uber, Airbnb, and Instagram—these businesses came from a generation of entrepreneurs who anticipated something in the zeitgeist."

To anticipate the zeitgeist, leaders have to know their audience. "That means digging deeper on data and constantly challenging your assumptions and the assumptions of your industry," Zalaznick said. For the Bravo network, it was Zalaznick's identification of a growing audience of affluent, educated, aspirational viewers interested in food, fashion, beauty, design, and pop culture. These five elements were the pillars that came to define Bravo's brand proposition and helped to ensure that every show produced by the network connected with its target audience.

"The most successful businesses win by anticipating or accelerating changing ethos in the zeitgeist," Zalaznick said. "The economic rebound from the original dot-com crash; the fatigue with the traditional genres of network comedies and dramas that were giving way to unscripted 'reality' television; and the growth of digital, viral communication all fueled our vision for growth."

CHALLENGING YOUR ASSUMPTIONS

Media is full of tropes and traps about consumers that don't stand up to scrutiny, said Zalaznick. "People in our industry love to say that young people today have shorter attention spans than they did in the past, and that's a potential disruptive force for our content," Zalaznick said. "But young people marathoning a whole series at a time on Netflix flies in the face of that logic."

Zalaznick's advice? Dig deeper. "Let's say it's true that young people are watching shorter and shorter content, but they are also watching more and more of it. That knowledge is going to change the calculus of how you approach the issue." In any competitive industry, "the quicker you take on the mantra of what everyone else is saying, the quicker you'll fail," Zalaznick said. "Don't fall into that trap."

MEASURING YOUR RISK BEFORE PLACING YOUR BET

Innovation is always a gamble. With limited resources to invest, leaders have to make strategic decisions about where to place their bets. To guide these decisions during her time at NBCU, Zalaznick plotted possible business-growth plays on a grid with four quadrants. In one quadrant she plotted opportunities that were easy to execute with a big expected payoff, an obvious yes. In another, she plotted opportunities that were hard to execute with little topline benefit, an obvious no. The two remaining quadrants—challenging but with a potentially big payoff, and easy to execute with a small but likely upside—were where most innovations fell. Those ended up being the critical decisions that drove the businesses.

"When you're dealing with uncertainty, there is no such thing as a sure thing," Zalaznick said. "It's up to the leader to make the best call using the information they have, with input from their team."

Leaders have to be prepared for investments that don't pan out. For example, Zalaznick said, in trying to capture viewers interested in social watching, NBCU acquired the second-screen app developer Zeebox and doubled down on creating their own app innovations to pair with their hit series. But the network later found that the viewers they were targeting were already interacting on Twitter and Facebook and preferred the aggregate experience of a centralized hub to individualized apps.

"In any industry, failure is going to happen," Zalaznick said. "It's what you learn from the failure that matters." The most important thing, Zalaznick said, is to create an environment where failure is not considered fatal and where solutions that challenge the status quo are given airtime and debated.

"Every employee should have a stake in innovation and feel empowered to bring new ideas to the fore," Zalaznick said. "Leaders are responsible for building a culture of innovation throughout every division rather than concentrating that responsibility in a single 'innovation team.'"

CREATIVITY AND DIVERSITY

One critical—and often overlooked—driver of innovation in business is diversity. "Many people are focused on the political value of diversity," Zalaznick said, "but there is a tremendous value for business, proven over and over again, in teams that can view a single issue through a variety of lenses—whether that's age, gender, race, culture, or background."

Diverse perspectives illuminate different approaches and offer insights into the preferences of an increasingly heterogeneous consumer base. And just as important as a diversity of perspectives, Zalaznick said, is a diversity of strengths. When assembling a team, she advised, leaders should seek out individuals with different but complementary skills.

"If you have eight direct reports and seven of them are 'drivers,' you've got challenges," Zalaznick said. "In every position, you need a person whose personality and skills are the right match for the task. For argument's sake, let's imagine that—in general—a person who needs a lot of information and rigor to make a decision is going to make a great general counsel and a terrible CMO, because a CMO sometimes needs to take very little information and act on it very quickly. But if you have them together on a team, they will complement and influence each other in the areas where each is lacking."

THE MOST INNOVATIVE LEADERS ARE TRUE TO THEMSELVES

If diverse teams drive creativity, that raises the question, does every member of the team have to be creative? According to Zalaznick, the answer is no.

"There's an ongoing debate about whether creativity is an innate or a learned skill," Zalaznick said. "But the fact is, there are many, many successful people who are deeply uncreative but who have myriad other talents that have allowed them to advance. So if it doesn't come naturally to you, it doesn't have to be your goal."

It's also important to remember, Zalaznick said, that creativity can come in many forms. "You can apply creativity in all aspects of your life. You can be creative in how you approach your career, in where you choose to live, and in the kinds of jobs you seek out. "I went from movies to TV, from marketing to programming, from a big network to a small network, and then from TV to digital. Not many people do that. I disrupted myself, and the result was a highly creative career."

To succeed and be happy and satisfied in the process, Zalaznick said, be true to yourself and know your strengths. "Being the best version of yourself and finding a company and management team that values you is more important than trying to be what everyone else is."

DR. JUDITH RODIN

Dr. Judith Rodin is President of the Rockefeller Foundation, a century-old philanthropic institution that works around the world to promote the well-being of humanity. She previously served as President of the University of Pennsylvania, where she oversaw a decade of growth that restored the university's place atop the rankings.

Dr. Rodin has made history many times in her career, becoming the first woman president of an Ivy League institution and then the first woman president of the Rockefeller Foundation. During her extraordinary tenure at the foundation thus far, she has redefined and renewed its strategy and program work after a period of relative stagnation— stewarding the foundation through its centennial and now into its second century. Dr. Rodin has authored hundreds of academic papers and written several books, including *The Resilience Dividend: Being Strong in a World Where Things Go Wrong*. She has been honored three times as one of "The World's 100 Most Powerful Women" by *Forbes*.

One of civil society's premier turnaround artists, Dr. Rodin shared her advice for developing resilient businesses, cities, and leaders. She explained the difference between role-modeling and mentorship ("Mentorship is a two-way process") and her approach to fostering innovation ("Safe failure is really important"). Her deep insight and resilient, innovative leadership inspires each of us to challenge the status quo.

In your wonderful new book, *The Resilience Dividend*, you powerfully argue that resilience is essential for institutions and communities. Is it possible for leaders to learn resilience?

Resilience is not an innate trait. It is a skill. It can be learned, developed, honed, and practiced.

This is incredibly important to understand because we often find that the media talks about resilience as if it is something you're lucky enough to be born with. That's not true. It's not purely a genetic trait.

How can individual leaders train themselves and their organizations to become more resilient?

In my book, I talk about the five characteristics of resilience that I believe are equally true whether you're an individual, a government, or a business.

The first characteristic is awareness. This means developing the skill and the capacity to be continuously aware in real time of what's going on around you. It also means having the critical faculties to assess all that information. It's why data analytics are so important. It's why every effective leader ought to have monitoring, measuring, and analytic units assisting him or her to help make real-time decisions and gather real-time intelligence. Awareness is absolutely critical.

The second characteristic is diversity or redundancy. In a time when businesses often feel like they are financially crunched, there has been a lot of emphasis placed on efficiency and cutting out every redundancy. But if you take that too far, you risk weakening your organization's resilience.

If you're an individual thinking about your own characteristics and skills, you want diversity in opinions. You want a breadth of insights, because it gives you a reinforced and diverse set of perspectives.

The third characteristic is being what we call self-regulating—the capacity to quickly cut off what's failing and going wrong. I like to say that it's better to fail safely rather than catastrophically. It's not that you can't fail, but there's a difference between failing safely and failing catastrophically. During Hurricane Sandy, there was no reason why one bad generator should have taken down all of lower Manhattan. There is something called smart-switch technology that allows you to delink the bad piece as soon as it fails. Having that would have been crucial.

The fourth characteristic is integration. When you're getting diverse sources of information, you need to integrate them effectively to understand what that means for yourself or your business. Having awareness alone is really not enough. It's about building your own capacity and the capacity of your business or your government to really integrate effectively along lots of lines of inputs. It's also why we love big-data analytics for decision making so much. But it's also important to know how to do this integration inside your own head.

The fifth characteristic is adaptability. A resilient leader, a resilient business, a resilient city is nimble. It's flexible. It can adapt in real time.

With those five characteristics, every young leader, business, and government can make themselves and all of their stakeholders more resilient.

You've spoken insightfully about the difference between being an effective mentor and being an effective role model. Can you talk about what mentoring and role modeling means to you personally?

I had amazing mentors once I got to Penn as an undergraduate. I was very lucky to have been singled out quite early in my freshman year in a psych class and then offered a job in a superstar faculty member, Dick Solomon's, lab. All four years, he and his graduate students mentored me. To me, that is the most profound mentoring relationship there is—when you're in a scientific discipline and your students become your partners.

In addition, while I was at Yale, I also had great mentors. I was actually among the first cohort of women faculty because I came to Yale the first year they admitted a full four-year class of women, which was in 1972.

But while I had great mentors, I had very few role models. There were very few women in positions of leadership—and the very few women who were ahead of me almost uniformly pulled up the ladder behind them. They did not help the women of my generation succeed.

From my generation on, I think women, in particular, have felt more of an obligation to be both mentors and role models. I've been really fortunate to be viewed as a role model. That means people I don't even know are looking at me and admiring the things I've achieved.

But what I value more about being a mentor is that it's a two-way process. If you're really mentoring, you're talking about things that make you anxious, about what you thought you did wrong and how you made tough decisions. You're not just standing on some pedestal—which is the pinnacle of role modeling.

Speaking of mentorship, one of your most impressive and enduring legacies is the enormous number of your former vice presidents, deans, and deputies—at both the University of Pennsylvania and the Rockefeller Foundation—who have gone on to lead prominent institutions of their own. Where, in your view, does mentorship fit in the roles and responsibilities of a leader?

I really think that when you're a CEO, part of your responsibility is to mentor and develop your talent. And there are few things more rewarding than watching your deputies ascend to prominent leadership positions.

When I took on the presidency at Penn, I made an effort to build a talented team of deans and senior officers, and now eight or nine of them have gone on to become university presidents themselves—one of my proudest accomplishments.

I've done the same at the Rockefeller Foundation. My former vice presidents and program leaders have gone on to lead institutions like the Ford Foundation, the Nonprofit Finance Fund, the Vera Institute for Justice, and the Century Foundation. The list goes on and on. I pride myself on that.

You are renowned as an innovative leader. Everywhere you've been, you've embodied change. Everywhere you've been, you've enabled it. How do you define innovation?

I've come to learn that there are several different kinds of innovation, and they're all equally important to understand and try to promote as a leader.

The most common understanding of innovation is what we usually think of in respect to a new product. This is the lightbulb-going-off moment or the aha moment that results in a new product outcome. But there are also other kinds.

There is process innovation, where you're really innovating around new ways of doing something.

There's organizational innovation, where you're organizing yourselves in different ways that promote different outcomes.

And there's market-based innovation, which we're doing with the field of impact investing, where you create new tools and metrics that, in turn, unlock new investment.

How do you create a culture of innovation and creative thinking, especially in a hundred-year-old organization that was founded on some very worthy principles but could be in danger of becoming too comfortable in its definition of its mission?

I think that's a critical point. When you've succeeded over a long period of time, it is human nature to get comfortable. And when you're a philanthropist and you're giving away money, people are not going to be as willing to tell you that you're not on your A game anymore. When I joined the Rockefeller Foundation, I didn't challenge what they were doing and how successful it was, because I felt that would be very countercultural to a proud legacy institution.

> "You have to create an environment where it's safe to fail. Safe failure is really important. To get real innovation, make it safe to experiment, to take smart risks, and to fail."
>
> —DR. JUDITH RODIN

Instead, I told the senior team that if we wanted to double our impact, we could not keep believing that everything was wonderful the way it is. We needed to ask ourselves how we could make positive changes. This made people think of new ways to innovate.

The second thing is, you have to create an environment where it's safe to fail. Safe failure makes it safe to experiment, to take smart risks, and to fail.

The third thing is having really effective, ongoing, real-time monitoring, because then you know what is and what isn't working and how it's working. That way you can make midcourse corrections. You can think about things in new ways.

And the fourth is to open yourself up to more people with more ideas—which in our case meant looking around the world.

We've completely transformed the way we get our ideas. We used to just assemble a smart program team and brainstorm. Now we have a process we call "scan," as in scanning the globe, where we engage global experts from around the world. This process forced us to acknowledge that not all great ideas live inside the Rockefeller Foundation.

During your tenure as the President of the University of Pennsylvania, you were responsible for rescuing the Penn Health System, which was on the verge of financial collapse. Unlike many of its counterpart universities, the Penn system is unique in that the hospital

and the medical school are fully integrated into the university, both financially and structurally. Talk to us about your approach. How did you resolve this crisis?

This crisis occurred during my third and fourth years. It defined my presidency. I had even written a resignation letter and put it in my drawer, just in case.

The health system had gone on a buying spree before the crisis occurred. After it hit, we were tens of millions of dollars in the red and on a trajectory to do worse the next year. The hospital's failure not only had the real threat of taking the health system down, but also of taking the university down with it.

The idea was that selling the hospitals would stop the bleeding, protect the medical school, and protect the rest of the university. We heard a few pitches from investment bankers and received proposals from some private companies, but after discussing it with my team, we decided not to do it. We were the first teaching hospital in America. We own Pennsylvania Hospital, which was America's first hospital. This was about more than our balance sheet. It was about our legacy, our brand, our pride, and our purpose as an institution.

We assembled a committee made up of faculty and trustees, and everyone worked together, pulling in the same boat with a coordinated set of oars. I was the coxswain with the executive vice president of the university at the time. We had to make a lot of changes. Our goal was to get rid of the excess. We knew we weren't going to sell the hospitals, but we really had to downsize.

In order to do that, I had to make an extraordinarily hard decision. I had to ask the dean and CEO of the health system to step down, even though he had tremendous support from many members of the board. I made sure I had the support of my board chair, and we brought in outside advisers to look at how to cut expenses in all of the hospitals. There wasn't one single thing we needed to do. We needed to do a thousand small things, and quickly.

Ultimately we were able to save the health system as part of a larger effort to revitalize the university and the larger community—West Philadelphia—of which it is part. It cost me about half the stack of chips that every leader gets when she starts, and I lost some leverage with some trustees that I never regained. But it was worth it for the sake of my alma mater, my hometown, and one of the largest employers in the state.

As President of the University of Pennsylvania and later the Rockefeller Foundation, you invested significant time in rethinking organizational strategy—a crucial precursor to your success. As a psychologist by training, however, you also have a better appreciation than most for the importance of organizational culture. How do you think about the interplay between strategy and culture? How can leaders ensure that each reinforces the other?

I think you have to keep iterating between culture and strategy. Great strategies get killed if there are cultural antibodies. You can't turn a ship with only a strategy. Great cultures can often hold you back if they're not agile enough to go with you to new places.

At Rockefeller, we talked a lot about iterative strategy. We learned a lot by trying things. We ultimately had to let a lot of people go after about a year. That's the iterative part—where you're implementing the strategy and trying to move the culture. If you find that the antibodies are too strong, then selective pruning is critical, and you have to be brave enough to do that.

It's very difficult. You need to do a gut check because no CEO takes letting people go lightly. But when you do it, it lifts the whole organization because the good people in the organization know who is dragging them down.

Finally, in light of everything we've discussed, if you could share one piece of advice—one kernel of wisdom—with young leaders in the first few chapters of their careers, what would it be?

For one thing, remember that it's about the quality, not the quantity of what you say. But more importantly, you must be your own worst critic and your own best fan. You shouldn't be one without the other, but the combination is really important.

JON M. HUNTSMAN, SR.

J on M. Huntsman, Sr., is the Founder and Executive Chairman of Huntsman Corporation, a multibillion-dollar global manufacturer and marketer of specialty chemicals. He is also a renowned philanthropist and a former leader and operative in the United States Republican Party.

Born to a modest family in rural Blackfoot, Idaho, Huntsman attended the University of Pennsylvania's Wharton School of Business on an academic scholarship and went on to found Huntsman Container Corporation in 1970. During the decades that followed, he oversaw Huntsman Corporation's transformation from a fledgling packaging operation to the nation's largest family-owned and family-operated business and one of the world's largest chemical companies. Huntsman Corporation went public in 2005, and today it is managed by Jon's son, Peter Huntsman, with annual revenues in excess of $10 billion.

For all of his success in business, Huntsman is perhaps just as well known for his philanthropy. A four-time cancer survivor, he has raised and donated more than $1 billion to cancer research and founded the Huntsman Cancer Institute in Utah, the world's largest cancer research center specializing in both adult and children's genetic cancers.

Huntsman explained his deep commitment to philanthropic work and the challenges and rewards that come with it. He shared his approach to innovation ("Basic can still be creative") and his rules for managing a successful family business ("Always be each other's best cheerleaders"). His energy, passion, and profoundly generous spirit can inspire all of us to devote our life's work to enhancing the greater good.

You have a wonderful, important new book out called *Barefoot to Billionaire*, in which you reflect on your lifetime of entrepreneurship—on your own American dream. Part of your success, of course, is innovation. Your invention of the Styrofoam egg carton in the 1960s revolutionized the industry, and since then, Huntsman Corporation has invented more than thirty popular commercial and household products. Talk to us about your philosophy. How do you think about innovation at Huntsman Corporation?

I've always felt—even back forty and fifty years ago when we were making products that were very basic to the American and world public—that our products had to be innovative and creative. They had to have some type of innovation that no one else had; otherwise our competitors could easily jump right in and, with the same amount of money or less, replicate our inventions and put us out of business. Today we produce over twenty-five thousand products that provide the materials for virtually everything we see, feel, wear, and touch, from airplanes, to paint, to running shoes, to toothpaste.

What inspired you to innovate in this space?

When I was in my twenties, I used to walk up and down the aisles of grocery and drug stores and merchandise marts and think of all the products that could be made from plastic. I wanted to see which of those products could be shifted over from glass or wood or paper and be made more cheaply and more lightly and more sustainably out of plastics. And that was the driving force behind what we did. It wasn't easy—the equipment we needed didn't exist yet, so we had to develop all of our own machinery as we went along.

But we plowed ahead in the early 1960s, first putting together the right equipment while making a lot of errors, but eventually we pulled together the first meat tray, the first egg cartons, the first Big Mac containers, and the first carryout food containers. Many of the early products that were made out of plastic were used in the fast-food business and then extended to other types of businesses. But for every product that ascended to the hall of fame—so to speak—there were just as many that ended up in the junkyard. We didn't hit a home run on everything, but we did well enough that we were able to produce hundreds of products that helped position us as major players in the plastics industry.

One of the principles of leadership is the ability to determine when it's most effective to lead from the front, lead alongside, or lead from behind. In fostering this culture of innovation, what kind of leadership did you exercise? Were you out there pushing your team to innovate in a certain direction, or was it more about giving them the permission to test out new ideas on their own?

We always led from the front; we could never lead from behind or beside. We had to create the right product at the right moment, and that meant being more hands-on in terms of direction. If we knew that somebody else was working on something, we had to stay up all night, whatever was necessary to stay ahead. The minute we tried to play catch-up ball, we were in a real jam, so we'd never allow ourselves to do that.

That isn't to say we were the lead one out on everything, but on most of the products that we came out with, we were the first ones to introduce it in the world. They were simple things; they weren't complex. But they were products that are still used today by the millions. And we did our best to ensure that, when we put them out, we were the first ones on the block.

Like The Estée Lauder Companies, Huntsman Corporation is a family business. The company carries your name, its first board of directors was comprised of your children, and your son Peter currently serves as president and CEO. How did you discourage and diffuse competition among family members working in the business?

We had two rules that everybody followed. Number one was that we would always be each other's best cheerleaders. And number two was that we would leave our egos at the door. The minute a family member starts bringing their ego into decisions, the business is in trouble. And the minute someone stops rooting for a brother or sister and stops supporting their accomplishments, we've lost the whole element of teamwork.

Did you set any other rules for your children prior to joining the family company, like, for example, mandating that they could join, but only after trying something else out for a period of time? Or requiring them to develop certain skills to ensure they were bringing the right value to the business?

I've always felt our children should have basic banking or finance experience before they go into any phase of business. Three or four of our children went on after school and spent two or three years working for major banks in New York.

> "My pursuit of the American Dream has been a made-in-America entrepreneurial journey of risk, reward, and tumult. I literally bet the farm on business deals that were economically akin to drawing inside straights. My company and I have been through more than one perfect storm. I kept the faith and won far more battles than I lost. I love to read—and on one occasion I came across the Edward R. Murrow expression that states, 'Difficulty is the one excuse history never accepts.' That bit of advice stayed with me during those devastating storms."
>
> —JON M. HUNTSMAN, SR., *BAREFOOT TO BILLIONAIRE*

But at a minimum, I insisted everyone who joined the business know two things: how to write and read the Queen's English and how to count the beans—how to read a balance sheet. Short of those two things, everything else can be learned on the job. So I took great pains to make sure those two areas—English and accounting—were basic knowledge for all of our children.

How did you manage the variation in talent and skills?

Not everyone is equal. Some of our children came out as superstars and were very bright when it came to academics. Others weren't as adept at school, but I would take them out on the road with me to call on accounts and they were absolute naturals in that area of the business. One of our children became very good at driving the truck. Another one took care of all of our warehouses, and there were others in our personnel department. It takes all kinds to run a big business like ours, and there are many different ways to contribute. Not everyone is made to be CEO. Which is a good thing, because there can only be one.

You've made social responsibility the heart of your mission at the Huntsman Corporation. How do you think about the role your company plays in society?

It's a sad commentary on the world today that many shareholders are only interested in the return on their investment and their stock and dividends. Everything revolves around quarterly earnings, and I think we've lost some focus on the greater good business can do for society.

We were private, much like The Estée Lauder Companies, for thirty-five years—and they were great years. I could take $300 million, $400 million, $500 million a year and put it into cancer research, public health, homelessness—and I had the time of my life doing that; it was so rewarding.

And then we went public ten years ago, and it put the brakes on some of what we did, because everything's scrutinized and transparency is critical. Public companies today have to be extremely careful about how they spend their money, and that's removed some of the enjoyment and spontaneity out of existing in public companies—for instance, being able to give things, do things, lift people, and serve the underserved.

> **"I made a lot of money in the second half of my life and formulated a plan for the end possessor of that fortune: to distribute it to good causes. I want to give it away—all of it— before I check out. I desire to leave this world as I entered it— barefoot and broke."**
>
> —JON M. HUNTSMAN, SR., *BAREFOOT TO BILLIONAIRE*

Fortunately, we're still able to do much of that today because I set up a foundation some years ago. We're able to withdraw funds from our personal foundations without impacting our public resources. But that's a rare situation for most corporations today.

Talk to us a little more about your philanthropy. You've been a lifelong philanthropist and one of the most prominent supporters of cancer care and research in the world, a cause that is very important to all of us in the Lauder family. You once said, "Neither business nor philanthropy are for the faint of heart." Can you elaborate on that?

After thirty-four years of giving, I've come to the conclusion that charity work is not for everyone. The art of giving is almost impossible to teach and difficult to learn. You virtually have to be born with an instinct for charity. It has to be embedded in your DNA.

That has always been the case for me. Giving brings joy to my heart. It's something that has brought us tremendous happiness. But it's not easy work. Just like in business, wherever there is money involved there are going to be people who are unhappy with the choices of how it's being spent.

Somebody is always upset with philanthropists because either one didn't receive funding for their charity, or eventually it became necessary to terminate funding at a certain point because our objectives were not being met, or we no longer had the resources to continue. In many ways, it's not unlike a business. If you establish a business and are successful, it can put a strain on certain relationships.

So if charity work is not something that comes naturally, one could easily become discouraged or cynical about it. But if one can overcome that and find the joy in giving, there is no work in this world that is more rewarding.

If you could share one piece of advice—one kernel of wisdom—with young leaders in the first few chapters of their careers, what would it be?

Don't ever give up on your dream, and don't be afraid to hire people who are stronger and smarter than you are to help you achieve your goal. Don't be risk averse, and above all else, set a tone in your company of hope, kindness, and integrity.

TRANSFORMATION

TRANSFORMATION

In today's business environment, the only certainty is uncertainty. A great leader understands the nature of change and is able to adapt quickly to new realities—even when that means transforming a long-successful business model.

Leading transformation isn't easy. Humans, by our nature, are resistant to change. And generating buy-in is hardest when business is booming and a threat to the status quo seems distant. That's why transformation is often best led in partnership and why crisis remains one of the best catalysts for change. Indeed, wise leaders never let a good crisis go to waste.

Fabrizio was that partner for me, and the 2008 financial crisis provided the momentum we needed to accelerate change at The Estée Lauder Companies. The same was true for Bill Ford, Executive Chairman of Ford Motor Company, who partnered with President and CEO Alan Mulally and used the automotive crisis to refocus the company on fuel efficiency and innovation.

For Michael Eisner, who transformed the Walt Disney Company from faltering film studio to global entertainment empire, change was the only option. With the company in an eighteen-year slump, Michael's vision and quick success earned him the trust and buy-in he needed to drive transformation.

And in an industry marked by rapidly evolving consumer tastes, PepsiCo Chairman and CEO Indra K. Nooyi sees transformation as the only constant. Since she joined the company more than two decades ago, she has been the driving force behind the diversification of PepsiCo's portfolio and the architect of its vision for sustainability.

Each of these examples illustrates that even—and perhaps especially—the world's most established companies are not immune to change. The best leaders know how to change tack without changing terminus—to keep a company agile and flexible, without losing sight of, or momentum toward, long-term strategic goals.

WILLIAM CLAY FORD, JR.

THE NEXT HUNDRED YEARS

William Clay Ford, Jr., Executive Chairman of Ford Motor Company, helped shepherd his great-grandfather's business through two of the toughest challenges in its century-long history: a dramatic restructuring and the most recent auto-industry crisis.

Today, Ford Motor Company is built like the cars it sells: tough, and for the long run. At the company's headquarters in Dearborn, Michigan, the balance sheets are healthy; labor costs have improved; and the R&D pipeline is flowing fast. Not to mention, Ford is the only major American automaker that didn't accept a federal bailout during the finanical crisis.

But skies weren't always blue for Ford's iconic Blue Oval.

In 2003, Ford celebrated the centennial of its founding. And according to Bill Ford, the company's chairman and CEO at the time, "there were storm clouds gathering on the horizon." "I had this nagging thought in my head," Bill recounted. "'What are our next hundred years going to look like?'"

That "nagging thought" led to the greatest leadership test of his career. During the past decade, Bill has helped shepherd Ford not only through the largest restructuring in company history, but also the largest crisis in the history of the auto industry.

IF IT AIN'T BROKE, DO FIX IT

For one thing, Bill said, effective leaders know how to recognize when a company needs to change, even if others can't.

By the time Bill ascended to the post of CEO, Ford—like the entire domestic auto industry—had "a lot of overcapacity." The company had built too many plants, signed uncompetitive labor agreements, neglected R&D, and even invested in the dot-com bubble. Their margins had begun to shrink by the mid-2000s as a result.

As Bill put it, "Our company had made at least twenty years of bad management decisions that I thought were about to come home to roost."

But there was an even bigger problem: Bill was among the few who could see that something was wrong under Ford's hood, so to speak. Big sales of big vehicles were masking the company's underlying financial vulnerabilities.

In 2006, Ford SUVs and trucks were moving off dealer lots in huge numbers. The company had just finished a run of highly profitable years. And not too far in the rearview mirror, 1999 stood out as the best year in Ford's history.

It was no surprise, then, that Ford's senior leadership team was less than responsive to any proposal to restructure the company.

As Bill pointed out, there can be "a lot of hubris in an insular industry and town." And Ford's single-industry town was no exception.

Many in the C-suite, after all, had risen through the ranks by helping to create the company that Bill said needed changing. So, one of his first dilemmas as a leader was—in his words—"convincing my company that we needed to go in a very different direction in the face of very good profitability."

To adapt the old cliché, Bill had to show that even though Ford wasn't broke, he still had to fix it. And he did so by taking bold action.

In 2006, he led the development of the strategy to mortgage the entire company, including the Blue Oval. This gave the company a $23 billion line of credit that would fund the restructuring. No company in history had ever borrowed more.

In the days after the loans, critics both inside and outside the company, including Chrysler and GM, thought Ford had "lost its collective mind." But months later, when the financial crisis struck and the credit markets froze, Bill was vindicated. And Ford had the capital it needed to survive the recession and emerge as a stronger company.

In other words, Ford's big bet succeeded far beyond most people's expectations.

WHEN STEPPING UP MEANS STEPPING BACK

But cash, of course, isn't all that's required to transform a company. It takes the courage of conviction-driven leadership, too.

To his credit, Bill Ford realized early on that sometimes the best way to lead a company is to let someone else lead it instead.

In 2006, before the financial crisis hit, Bill served as Ford's chairman, CEO, president, COO, and even—he jokes—as its "chief car washer." By his own admission, he was wearing "too many hats" and needed help.

And that's exactly what he told his board of directors. "What's coming at us looks like a tidal wave," he said, "and I've got nobody, including myself, who's ever done a restructuring on the scale that I think we're going to need."

Sometimes, Bill knew, in order to step up, you also have to step back. So Ford's board quietly began the search for a new CEO, one with the right experience, talent, and temperament to transform a global corporation of 280,000 employees. And they landed on Alan Mulally.

Mulally had impeccable credentials and references who sang his praises. A former engineer, he had led Boeing's restructuring after September 11, 2001, when the commercial aircraft industry was brought to a halt and the company lost 60 percent of its sales in one year.

In the summer of 2006, Mulally met Bill to discuss coming on board. Bill was immediately impressed. Alan was focused on guiding the company, not ordering it on a forced march. "Within an hour," Bill said, "we were finishing each other's sentences."

On September 5, 2006, Alan Mulally was named President and CEO of Ford Motor Company.

Bill had done a rare thing. He'd placed the well-being of the company ahead of his title. And his humility paid off: he found a partner to restructure the company.

"And then," Bill recalled, "the world started to fall apart."

KEEPING THE COMPANY—AND THE CULTURE—ALIVE

Ninety-nine years ago—at a time when the average worker earned two dollars a day—Bill's great-grandfather Henry Ford decided to pay his employees more. Workers on the Ford assembly lines in Detroit began to take home five dollars a day, and some even shared company profits.

Over the past century, this commitment to corporate social responsibility—this bridging of the gap between labor and management—has become the Ford Motor Company's creed. And Bill Ford believes deeply in it. After all, Bill said, he joined the company out of college and worked on the assembly line. He still lives close to Detroit.

"My family has always been a part of the community," Bill said. "I care deeply about the people who are there. And I don't want to let them down."

That's why mere survival wasn't Ford's goal when the bottom fell out of the market in 2007, pushing American auto companies to the brink of bankruptcy.

"A company's survival isn't enough if it doesn't survive with the same ethics and culture that made it different and special."

There were many factors that would determine if Ford could survive in that way, but two stood out as particularly important.

The first factor was whether Ford could—or even should—maintain its independence. Between 2007 and 2008, the White House put heavy pressure on Ford to merge with GM "for the good of the country."

When the Ford leadership team performed its due diligence, they found there were too many redundancies—and too few synergies—between Ford and GM. The merger would not have created jobs. On the contrary, Bill said: "By the end of the day, it would've shrunk the combined entity down to something that looks a lot like one of the companies today."

So, Bill, Alan, and the board decided that Ford could—and would—remain an autonomous corporation.

But the company still had to contend with a second factor: labor. If Ford was to survive, it needed to renegotiate its contracts with its workers and retirees.

Here Bill faced another dilemma: How could he do the greatest good for the most people knowing that he was going to hurt some people?

Bill knew that whatever the answer, labor needed to come along. So he approached Ron Gettelfinger, the head of the United Auto Workers. Gettelfinger understood immediately that although the renegotiation would be painful, there wasn't any other way around it. The auto workers relied on Ford just as much as Ford relied on the auto workers.

Gettelfinger gave Bill his word, pledging, "I'll do anything I can to make sure that you guys survive and succeed." And he did. Gettelfinger negotiated within his union to secure the contracts necessary for Ford to survive. In Bill's words, "the United Auto Workers were absolutely heroic."

In partnership with organized labor, the Ford Motor Company made it through the auto crisis and, today, operates with low labor costs. Just as importantly, the company is still delivering the benefits their employees and retirees have earned.

Simply put, Ford didn't just survive; its culture did, too.

EMERGING FROM CRISES STRONGER

The cliché "every crisis presents an opportunity" is well worn. But Bill Ford's story offers a new twist on an old standby.

On the eve of Ford's restructuring, Bill said, he had a memorable conversation with Alan Mulally. "There's no point in going through all the pain we're about to go through if there's no light at the end of the tunnel," Bill told Alan. "If we just come out looking like the same old Ford Motor Company, then this isn't worth the trip."

Which leads to Bill's final lesson: companies should emerge from existential crises stronger—or not at all.

It was that kind of confidence that guided Ford's senior leadership team as it worked to transform the company. "We decided," Bill said, "we would double down on two things which had been weaknesses for us."

The first weakness was fuel economy.

Before 2007, studies showed that poor fuel economy had been the number one reason that car shoppers refused to buy Ford cars. Today, however, Ford has turned one of its greatest weaknesses into one of its greatest strengths, offering a variety of power train choices across its lineup to best meet its customers' vehicle needs, their lifestyles, and their fuel-efficiency demands. These choices range from the popular EcoBoost-powered gasoline vehicles to hybrids, plug-in hybrids, and full electric vehicles.

The second weakness was innovation.

Years before crisis struck the auto industry, Japanese and European manufacturers had established themselves as the cutting-edge leaders in technology, on the dashboard and under the hood. Ford, on the other hand, had largely let its innovation pipeline slow to a trickle, much like GM and Chrysler.

But during the midst of the recession—as their competitors slashed R&D budgets to strengthen their balance sheets—Ford did the opposite. The company invested heavily to produce the next wave of entertainment technology and interface technology, like the in-car communications and entertainment systems Ford SYNC and MyFord Touch. While the first generation of this technology had bugs that needed to be addressed, 80 percent of Ford drivers still recommend their vehicles and the technology inside them. Ford SYNC is now in more than twelve million vehicles on the road globally, and the recently launched SYNC 3 is getting rave reviews.

Without a doubt Ford has emerged from its restructuring—and the financial crisis—stronger than ever. And more tech savvy, too. The light at the tunnel's end is bright.

THE FUTURE OF THE AUTO INDUSTRY

Ultimately, Bill remains focused on Ford's next hundred years. And that will mean more changes for the Blue Oval as the needs of society continue to evolve.

"I strongly believe that no company deserves to exist unless they're making people's lives better. And if they're not making people's lives better, they've probably run their course," Bill said.

Before the Model T, Bill explained, most Americans didn't travel more than twenty-five miles from home in their entire lifetime. "Looking back to my great-grandfather, what he did was he provided freedom of mobility to the average person. When the Model T came, all of a sudden people could choose where they lived, where they worked, and where they played. And it really changed everything. And Americans became mobile, and then ultimately the world became mobile."

The next challenge for the Ford Motor Company is to redefine that freedom of movement into an ever more crowded urban world—a world, Bill noted, that is facing rapidly increasing transportation problems.

As the population approaches nine billion by midcentury, Bill noted, "it could become a human rights issue if we're unable to move food and health care around major urban areas." These are problems Bill envisions Ford addressing in the coming years—problems that deal not only with cars, but with mobility writ large.

"If we don't do it, if we just stay with today's model, we will be, in twenty years, selling our cars only to people in rural areas and suburbanites. That's not terribly interesting, it's a lousy business model, and it doesn't solve anybody's problems. But if we can be a company that actually solves some of these issues, makes people's lives better, and stays relevant, we can remain in the vanguard of our industry."

"We just need to keep our place among the innovators," he said. "It will be technology that sets us free."

MICHAEL EISNER

Michael Eisner is a seasoned veteran of the entertainment industry and former Chairman and CEO of the Walt Disney Company. Eisner transformed the troubled film studio and amusement park business into a global entertainment powerhouse during his twenty-one-year tenure. Between 1984 and 2005, Eisner presided over a string of box office hits, including instant classics *The Little Mermaid, Beauty and the Beast,* and *Aladdin,* as well as Disney's lucrative acquisitions of the ABC and ESPN networks. The company, valued at just $1.8 billion when Eisner took over, was worth more than $80 billion upon his departure.

The empire Eisner built continues to flourish today. Disney currently operates eleven theme parks and forty-four resorts around the world, along with its own cruise line. It distributes a wide array of popular film, television, theater, and music programming.

Eisner described his strategy for managing a media empire, including his focus on synergy, weekly lunches with division heads, and a Disney "hell week" inspired by his college fraternity days. He shared the secrets of Disney's drastic turnaround ("It was amazingly easy") and the unique struggles that come with massive success ("You've got to do it every year"). Amid his wry humor and sharp observations are lessons in visionary leadership that can help all of us at The Estée Lauder Companies tap into our inner creativity.

The scale of Disney's operations is staggering—from a cruise line to a sports-television conglomerate—and you were responsible for keeping it all running smoothly. How did you manage such an expansive and diverse portfolio? How do you know when to step in and when to get out of the way?

In a word: synergy. It might sound like a buzzword, but for a company like ours, it was the driving force behind our success. Synergy is the key to leveraging a diverse portfolio of businesses to get the most out of every investment you make. And for me, synergy is synonymous with communication. So from day one, we started a tradition of weekly lunch meetings with the heads of each business unit. It was a significant commitment. No matter where they were in the world, on Mondays they were expected to be in our office for lunch. If a unit head couldn't be there, they sent a representative in their place, but without exception, every brand leader was represented at every meeting. Each one would talk about what they were doing that week, and if there were opportunities for synergy across our businesses, we would identify and capitalize on them.

Did you have a direct hand in coordinating those opportunities across the various divisions?

At first, yes. But when we got very big, it became more difficult for all the synergy to come up through the CEO. So we had to come up with an alternative strategy to bring people together. The result was Disney's version of "hell week."

It was an idea that came from my college fraternity days. Three times a year, we'd select twenty top people in the company and they'd spend eight days traveling the world visiting every division of the company.

Their days were scheduled from six in the morning until eleven at night with no phone calls allowed. If they were in the parks, they'd spend two hours with the financial operations, two hours in costume, three hours peeling potatoes in the hotel kitchen—everything there was to do, they experienced it. They'd spend another half a day at Disneyland and then a full day in the motion picture division having presentations of every film. They'd go to the labs. They'd spend days in television. They'd go to ESPN in Connecticut for a day, and to Paris, and to Japan.

They despised me for this. By the end of the eighth day, I was the common enemy. They all loved each other and hated me.

What did people learn after going through "hell week"? How did that experience translate to better synergy and better performance at the business level?

It was really a process of continual learning for the leaders in our company. For one thing, everybody appreciated that it wasn't easy to deliver millions of french fries a day at Walt Disney World. That experience gave people a little more respect for and insight into the work that goes into running our businesses at every level.

But the biggest shift was that after we started doing "hell weeks," the synergy no longer had to go up through me. Because people had built relationships with one another, it could happen on a parallel basis. So if we were doing a *Toy Story* movie, the guy at the park could just call the guy at the studio and say, "What kind of parade do you want?" The guy in consumer products could call ESPN and say, "What can you do at ESPN to promote the new park ride and the movie itself?"

The other thing we did to build unity was to create stock options that went through the corporation. So instead of the guy running the parks hoping the guy running the studio—who he thought made too much money—got run over by a truck, he actually rooted for that guy. The stock-option plan we created meant that any one person's success was a success for the whole.

When you joined Disney, the company was in an eighteen-year slump. Under your leadership, Disney did an about-face, growing into one of the nation's most profitable, successful, and best-loved companies. Looking back, what are some of the key decisions that led to the turnaround?

It was amazingly easy, actually. We had such a head start because of who we were as a company. Disney was still an iconic brand, all the fundamentals were still there, but since Walt Disney had died, the execution had been poor. There was so much low-hanging fruit there that all we had to do was take what Walt had created and run with it.

Disney hadn't developed any blockbuster IP since Walt had died, so we went out and made a deal with George Lucas for *Star Wars* and *Raiders of the Lost Ark,* which we put in our parks. That gave us a three-year head start before we started making our own hits.

After that, we set about making improvements in every area of the business. We upgraded the food at the parks. We went back into the movie business. We revolutionized the animation business with *The Little Mermaid, Beauty and the Beast,* and *Aladdin.* We stopped treating Disney as a kids' company and started putting out quality pictures that attracted adults, too. We revoiced all of our animated television outside the United States, which had been done really shoddily up to that point. We realized that the parks were substantially underpriced, so we raised ticket prices, and that move alone created an enormous economic windfall that funded many of the other improvements we wanted to make.

After eighteen years of mediocrity at Disney, how did you reignite the creative spark? How did you create a culture that fostered creativity over the long term?

It sounds simple, but you just have to be open to it. If you have a big organization, you already have creative people on hand. You just have to give them the platform and the opportunity. The problem is, management tends to stifle creative people and put them in a corner when they should actually be lionizing them.

> "If you have a big organization, you already have creative people on hand. You just have to give them the platform and the opportunity. The problem is, management tends to stifle creative people and put them in a corner when they should actually be lionizing them."
>
> —MICHAEL EISNER

My first week at Disney, I held a meeting with every person who was in charge of a creative piece of the company. These people had never, ever met with somebody high up at the company before. We all sat down for a few hours, and by the end of the meeting we had created two television shows and mapped out a whole new direction. You never know what can come from a small gesture like that. If you open the door and invite creativity in, you'll find there is no shortage of creativity out there.

In the entertainment industry, failure is a rite of passage, but success also brings its own set of challenges. What kind of challenges did you face once you were on top?

We had so much success so quickly that we were something of an overnight wonder for almost eighteen years. The problem is that dealing with success is actually much harder than dealing with failure. I was an expert at dealing with failure. I was at ABC when we were fourth among three, and we put on shows that nobody watched. So I knew how to deal with failure really well.

When we came to Disney, they had had an eighteen-year run of failure, so they were pretty good at dealing with failure as well. Then all of a sudden we were dealing with success. And that requires much more management skill.

Dealing with failure is easy. You cut 5 percent of your workforce; nobody complains. There are no bonuses; nobody complains. People are demoted; nobody complains. Nobody asks for a new contract because everybody is just thrilled that they're not on somebody's pink-slip list.

Success is the opposite. Everybody is a genius. Everybody wants new contracts. People get arrogant and opinionated, and that can lead to a lot of internal conflict.

Everybody says, "Boy, I'd really love to have that issue." And it is a great issue to have. But there's an added layer of pressure, too, because anybody can be successful once. One success is nothing. If you're in the movie business or the television business, you've got to do it every year.

You wrote a book called *Working Together* that is all about successful partnerships, including your partnership with the late Frank Wells at Disney. Talk to us a little about partnerships. What should leaders look for in a potential partner?

Partnerships are great because they're a check on your point of view. They can encourage you to take smart risks when you should, and save you from making major mistakes. It's also just a little bit more fun and a little less lonely when you're working with a partner.

The first thing to look for in a partner is a strong moral compass. You have to find somebody who errs on the side of morality, who has a strong sense of right and wrong, and who can tell you when something doesn't pass the smell test, even if everyone else is telling you it's a good move.

The second thing is compatibility. In many ways, a partnership is like a marriage, and just like with your spouse, you have to like the idea of being together every day, talking on the phone ten times a day, and traveling together constantly.

The third is a complementary skill set—a person who doesn't excel in all the same ways as you, but instead adds another dimension to your attributes. If it's the right complement, then the two of you together will add up to having a third person in the room.

The fourth is someone who questions everything—questions your decisions, questions your point of view, questions your financial risk taking, and then enhances and encourages your risk taking. I think leaders who don't have that eventually fail. They end up believing in their own worst ideas, and the ladder they climbed up quickly becomes a chute they go tumbling down.

Let's talk about recruiting and cultivating talent, because for a large organization, it's not just the brilliance and vision of the CEO that makes a company successful; it's all the people in the company who share the vision and execute it on a daily basis. How do you find, develop, and retain great talent?

I think it starts at the top—as I like to say, a fish stinks from the head. You've got to make sure that your CFO and your general counsel and your division heads are great. That piece is the CEO's responsibility. If those leaders are great, they will recruit great talent underneath them.

Big companies and brands with respect have an enormous advantage. The best and brightest from the top schools gravitate toward the big companies, and it's much harder for smaller companies to compete. When you have a great pool of candidates, as we usually did, then you're looking for things like vision, articulation, creativity, and ethics in new hires.

Retaining talent is trickier. You'll never have any trouble keeping executives when you fail. As a matter of fact, you can't get rid of them.

But when you're successful, everybody is looking at your company to poach. On one hand that's a compliment, and a certain amount of turnover is good, because it creates opportunities for upward mobility. But if you have great people you want to keep, you can't be afraid to pay well and create financial incentives that encourage them to stay on and continue performing.

If you could share one piece of advice, one kernel of wisdom to young future leaders in the first few chapters of their careers, what would it be?

Make it a practice to tell the truth. No matter how bad, or difficult, or unpleasant it is at times, if you always tell the truth, the people you work for will have tremendous confidence in you. If you can be a person of your word, that will go a long way toward a successful career.

A CONVERSATION WITH
INDRA K. NOOYI

Indra K. Nooyi is the Chairman and Chief Executive Officer of Pep-siCo, one of the world's leading food and beverage companies, with products enjoyed by consumers in more than two hundred countries and territories. She is the first woman to serve as the company's CEO, and she previously held positions as the company's President and Chief Financial Officer.

Before becoming CEO, Nooyi spearheaded several of the largest acquisitions in PepsiCo's history, bringing in Tropicana, Quaker Oats Company, and Gatorade to diversify PepsiCo's traditional portfolio of snack foods and soft drinks. She is also the chief architect of Perfor-mance with Purpose, PepsiCo's goal to deliver top-tier financial per-formance while creating sustainable growth and value that benefit shareholders and communities alike. She is regularly listed among the world's most powerful women by *Forbes, Fortune,* and other publica-tions.

As a Fortune 50 CEO, Nooyi explained how she divides her days to balance the demands of managing PepsiCo's portfolio of twenty-two billion-dollar brands and more than 270,000 employees. She discussed the cultural challenges associated with transforming a business and the inspiration behind Performance with Purpose. Her visionary lead-ership and relentless drive can motivate all of us to take charge and ownership of our own success in business.

PepsiCo is comprised of twenty-two billion-dollar brands and has products in more countries than the United Nations. As CEO, you're responsible for keeping it all running smoothly. How do you manage so many diverse projects and cultures? What's the secret to running a Fortune 50 company?

No CEO can run the whole company by themselves. The secret is to find the right people, to whom you know you can entrust parts of the company, and then to make sure that they, in turn, hire the right teams. As the companies get bigger and bigger, the CEO becomes more of the conductor of the orchestra rather than a person playing an instrument—although you should be able to step into a couple of the instrument chairs if you are so needed.

To do that, you need to understand every part of the business: What's the business model? What kind of partnerships do you have? What kind of relationships? What are the issues in the big markets? You need to get into the details and know what's going on, because when there is a problem and your executive comes to you for help, they can't educate you from scratch. You've got to have some baseline knowledge of what is going on at any given moment. You have to be willing to dig into the details when it's necessary and then move back out to let your people manage the business.

Walk us through your typical day. How do you divide your time?

In a typical day, I'd say 20 percent of my time is spent dealing with people issues: talking to people about their next task, giving them some feedback, helping them through some problem, or working on their development.

Another 20 percent is spent reading up on issues that are not directly about PepsiCo but have some impact on PepsiCo. It might be the latest political crisis, or it might be something related to health and wellness regulations or dietary guidelines—something that has an impact on the business but is not driving business day to day.

Another 30 percent is on meetings on big issues that impact the company in the future, and the final 30 percent is on detailed business operating reviews.

So while it varies by day of the week or month of the year, I'd say 20 percent on people; 20 percent on reading about broader world issues; 30 percent on longer-term issue meetings; and 30 percent on the nitty-gritty of today's operations is a pretty good breakdown of my day.

You led PepsiCo's transformation in the late 1990s and early 2000s from a chips-and-soda company to the world's premier food-and-beverage company, bringing iconic brands like Tropicana, Quaker, and Gatorade into PepsiCo's portfolio. Talk to us about your decision to expand and diversify PepsiCo's offerings. How did you know it was the right time to transform?

It really goes back to reading about issues, talking to people, and just looking around the world. I think people who didn't notice the health-and-wellness trend must have had their heads buried in the sand, because it was right in front of us for all to see. Because the great thing about our kind of business is that we are also consumers. Unlike a jet engine or power plant, where you're a very indirect consumer, in our business we are the direct consumer. And all we had to do was look around the room and see what our people were eating or drinking.

I saw that evolving over time in two ways. First, as people got older they were eating and drinking different products. And second, even the younger people were eating and drinking differently over time. I felt that the time had come for us to say, look, there's a time and place for treats, but there's also a time for more nutritious products. And if we want to stay competitive, we need to offer both.

One of your greatest contributions to PepsiCo has been a business philosophy that you created and implemented called Performance with Purpose—which is your vision for long-term, responsible, sustainable growth at the company. Where did this idea originate?

Performance with Purpose began as an effort to unite our businesses around a greater sense of purpose.

We're a high-performance company, and we know what the financial metrics are and what we need to deliver. But at the same time, we're mindful of what really motivates somebody on our team to get up in the morning and come to work.

I asked this question of young people and also of people who have been in the company fifteen or twenty years: What are you excited about? And it occurred to me that we needed to create a purpose for PepsiCo that people could connect with emotionally and take pride in. I wanted our associates to be able to say, "This is the company I want to come to work for, and for a larger purpose."

> "We're a high-performance company, and we know what the financial metrics are and what we need to deliver. But at the same time, we're mindful of what really motivates somebody on our team to get up in the morning and come to work."
>
> —INDRA K. NOOYI

What exactly does Performance with Purpose entail? How do you communicate and reinforce that with your team?

In addition to great performance, there are three planks that encapsulate this broader purpose.

First, everybody at PepsiCo knows that the consumer is changing. Our consumers are looking for healthier options to support a balanced diet. So the first part of our purpose is evolving our portfolio to meet that demand. We are finding ways to add more fruits and vegetables, grains, and protein in our offerings and at the same time working to reduce the fat, added sugar, and sodium in our products. That's plank one—human sustainability.

The second plank is environmental sustainability. We generate plastic waste. We use water in our operations. We have lots of trucks on the road. We have a big carbon footprint. Everybody wants to leave their children and grandchildren a better world. So we've asked ourselves, how can we reduce the waste that we generate? Not because it fulfills some corporate social-responsibility obligation, but because it's simply good business. We've saved a lot of money by reducing the amount of plastic we use, by recycling more, and by moving towards an all-electric fleet.

And the third plank is our people. PepsiCo has awesome talent, but the war for talent is fierce. How do we make our people feel like PepsiCo is a place where you can not only make a livelihood, but also have a life? I want our employees to bring their whole selves to work. I don't want them to feel like they are leaving themselves at the door when they come in every day. So we provide opportunities for our employees to pursue their passions beyond their day-to-day work. We help them develop new skills, explore new areas, and volunteer in the community so they can bring that energy back to everything we do as a company.

How has Performance with Purpose contributed to your success as a company?

Each of these planks powers our performance. Human sustainability helps drive our top line. Environmental sustainability helps us save money and secure our license to operate in society. Talent sustainability helps us attract the best and brightest.

Performance with Purpose is not CSR; it's part and parcel of our business. It's how we make our money, not how we spend the money we make.

Let's talk about the talent pipeline. PepsiCo is one of the most desirable companies to work for. So many top people, smart people in so many different disciplines. And PepsiCo has a reputation as the academy for so many great executives whose careers have been very successful both inside the company and when they've left PepsiCo. How do you attract and retain this top talent? What do you do from a cultural standpoint to foster this culture?

I was once having dinner with a very well-known media personality. And he had the following to say about PepsiCo, and I'll share it with you.

He said, "You know, Indra, when you think about PepsiCo, it is not a company. It is a culture. It's an ethos."

People come to PepsiCo saying, "You know what? I can actually be part of people's everyday lives." I can be part of their eating and drinking habits, which is fundamental to a culture, how people live, how people nourish themselves. So people who come to work at PepsiCo come for that reason. But they could leave. How do we hold on to them, and how do we move them forward?

I think within PepsiCo is a very youthful culture. It doesn't matter how old you are. Within PepsiCo, everybody is young. You talk to anybody at PepsiCo, it is amazing how they think young, act young—not immature—and they're all full of life. And even when they leave PepsiCo, first of all, they miss PepsiCo like you won't believe. They'll talk about PepsiCo all the time.

I think it's something about PepsiCo that grows on people, that gets into their blood. And they all bleed PepsiCo long after they leave. And there's a great sense of attachment to this company. And I think it's because, first, when they come here we treat them well. We give them extremely challenging assignments. Sometimes it's sink or swim, and they love it.

Because at the end of the day, if people in PepsiCo don't feel a sense of ownership about the company, who is going to? With my senior executives, if anybody says to me, "PepsiCo has to change," I go, "Who in PepsiCo has to change? Is it you?" So talk about it in the first person. Don't talk about it in the third person.

So by pushing people to own this company more and more and truly be passionately committed to this company, I think it's very infectious and transmits itself to the whole company. And we really, really make people feel like this is their company. So this ownership culture is fantastic.

Let's talk about mentorship. You've worked in a number of different enterprises and different industries. Who has mentored you throughout your life and career?

I've had some amazing mentors. But I honestly believe mentors pick you; you don't pick them. If you are really good, people will find you because they want to hitch their wagon to you. And I have been very lucky. From the time I was a very young executive working in India, somebody has always been willing to become my mentor.

I've had mentors who were my direct bosses or my boss' boss. They've been clients when I was at BCG who are still with me to this day. They've been CEOs at PepsiCo who preceded me and who still stay in touch. But they haven't all been senior people. Sometimes it's the security guard at PepsiCo who comes up to me and says, "Hey, Mrs. Nooyi, I just want to tell you this," and points out some issue that I wasn't aware of. If you're open to ideas, you'll find a lot of people who want to look out for you.

Even though I've never worked with him directly, Leonard A. Lauder has been a particularly great mentor to me. He is always very open with his advice and feedback. Sometimes it might hurt to hear in the short term, but once I process it, I always come back and say, "Wow, he is so damned right." And I always call him back and tell him what I did with his advice.

As a mentor now yourself, what advice would you give to mentees to make the most of the mentor-mentee relationship?

As a mentee, you have to be willing to take the feedback, however negative it might be, and make the appropriate changes to demonstrate that you're listening. If you get advice and you don't plan to take it, make sure you explain why. There's nothing more frustrating to a mentor than having their advice ignored.

Finally, in light of everything we've discussed, if you could share one piece of advice—one kernel of wisdom—with young leaders in the first few chapters of their careers, what would it be?

Don't think your learning has ended when you leave school. Your learning has only just begun. Your education in the university system may have ended, but your learning in a practical environment has just started.

You have to keep learning throughout the entirety of your career. I actually believe the higher up you move in a company, the more you have to learn, the more you have to read, the more you've got to go to a different kind of university. It's a university you create, a university that you set up for yourself in order to continue your own education.

THE ART OF THE PIVOT

LEADERSHIP SPOTLIGHT

James D. Robinson, IV

A CONVERSATION WITH

Laura Alber

THE ART OF THE PIVOT

Though few consumers realize it, many of the world's most beloved products were invented by accident. The Post-it Note was invented forty years ago by a chemist at 3M who—attempting to develop a high-powered adhesive—accidently produced a weak one instead. On the suggestion of a colleague, the chemist affixed the mild glue to the back of paper bookmarks and thus transformed a failed experiment into one of the most successful office products of all time.

Post-it Notes are just one of many successful pivots found throughout the history of business, and these stories offer a timeless lesson for leaders: you don't always accomplish what you set out to, but if you're flexible of mind, sometimes what you accomplish will be even greater.

For leaders—especially those in creative industries—it's important to recognize when opportunity lies in a pivot. Of course, not every failed experiment leads to innovation. Just as important as recognizing latent opportunity is the ability to differentiate between a business in need of course correction and a sinking ship. In the latter case, walking away is ultimately the right decision for the total enterprise.

This is the job of RRE Ventures Co-Founder Jim Robinson. Robinson's work requires a keen eye for potential as well as the judgment to make tough calls when it becomes apparent that a business is floundering. Much of his work involves guiding start-ups through course corrections as they navigate uncharted territory.

During Laura Alber's tenure at Williams-Sonoma Inc., the visionary president and CEO has led the company through a number of pivots to bring its brands and products to previously untapped markets—

including the world of high-end children's home furnishings, a significant departure from the company's initial offerings.

Their examples illustrate one of the most important ways leaders
add value to an enterprise: by using their unique insights and experience to keep the business moving forward and to ensure it's heading in
the right direction.

JAMES D. ROBINSON, IV

LEADING A PORTFOLIO OF COMPANIES

As co-founder and managing partner of tech-focused RRE Ventures, James D. Robinson, IV, oversees nearly $1.5 billion in VC investments. In the world of VC, every investment is a gamble.

"There is no spreadsheet you can make, no due diligence you can really do. We will talk to scientists and experts, of course, but ultimately, if you invest in venture, particularly if you're a lead investor and you invest early, you're in the tea-leaf-divination business," Robinson said.

RRE's model is to take a position in a nascent technology, what Robinson calls a "zero billion-dollar industry," and "hope like hell that it's going to be a really big industry tomorrow."

When the team strikes gold, the payoff can be huge. But for every winning bet, there are at least two that don't pan out. "It's really the law of thirds," Robinson said. "A third of investments do badly and lose most or all of your money. A third get some portion to maybe a couple of times your investment back, but over a time frame that isn't a particularly good returner. And the remaining third is where you make most or all of your money."

The single easiest way to lose money—in VC or in any business— says Robinson, is to follow sunk costs. Which is why, he said, it's critical that leaders know when to course correct and when to abandon ship.

AVOIDING THE TEMPTATION TO THROW GOOD MONEY AFTER BAD

In fact, RRE Ventures might not exist today had Robinson been unable to abandon an earlier enterprise.

After business school, Robinson started a company with a classmate. Their big idea was to install touch screens in the seats of stadiums and arenas across the country. The technology would allow spectators to order food and tickets to future events without missing any of the action.

Alas, their business was ahead of its time. Wi-Fi was yet to be invented. Few stadium managers were eager to see their flooring torn up in order to run cable for the touch screens.

Wisely, Robinson and his co-founder, Stuart Ellman, chose to abandon the idea after about six months, making a strategic decision to seek opportunity elsewhere. It was a smart move that led them, eventually, to establish their own venture capital fund, which, today, manages $1.5 billion of assets in information-technology companies.

After more than two decades in business, Robinson said, it's still a challenge to avoid throwing good money after bad. But effective leaders in any industry, he argued, intuit when to walk away from something in which they have already invested. They are shrewd, savvy, and strong enough to know when to cut their losses.

That doesn't mean it's easy to cut and run—especially from something you've worked on personally. As Robinson pointed out, it's not just money that goes into RRE's ventures. As lead investors, the fund's partners and associates invest significant time, energy, and emotion into each project and often develop personal relationships with leaders at the start-up.

"You're living side by side with, and often become quite close to, not just the founders and the CEO, but usually much of the senior team," Robinson said. "It is a very difficult thing when you've become friends— in some cases, your families become friends, maybe your kids become friends—when all of a sudden, something has happened and you've got to make some tough decisions."

One method that helps leaders maintain a clear and impartial lens on their own investments are self-imposed rules.

Imposing artificial rules can be helpful in guarding against a common pitfall in every industry: confirmation bias. Too often, business leaders who have been involved in an initial decision are too personally invested—emotionally and psychologically—to make a tough subsequent decision.

"It's really easy to hear those pieces of information that you're expecting to hear," Robinson said. "Rules can help leaders distance themselves from the value proposition they're evaluating and make better decisions as a result."

PERSONAL MATTERS MATTER

Of course, not all portfolio decisions can be made on a strictly strategic level. Relationships matter, too. And one critical aspect of maintaining a high-functioning business partnership is staying mindful of your colleagues' needs and interests.

Robinson always considers the relationships at play when he makes investment decisions within his firm—"HR issues that you don't necessarily think about but that matter a great deal."

For instance, when deciding whether to invest in a venture, Robinson considers his relationship with the partner pitching the idea in addition to the viability or potential of the investment itself.

"What I don't want," Robinson said of his relationship with his partners, "is to turn down a company or idea that you're championing today, and then three months, six months, nine months, two years from now, you're that much more inclined to turn down one that I'm championing—not based on the merits of the scenario but based on a memory of having been shot down." This is one of many reasons, said Robinson, that managing relationships within firms is "incredibly important."

PIVOTS AND COURSE CORRECTIONS

Oftentimes, Robinson said, a start-up comes to RRE with the right foundation for success but needs help adjusting its strategy. That's why effective leaders are skilled in the art of the pivot—the capacity to adapt with changing circumstances. After all, Robinson said, somewhere between 12 and 15 percent of the companies in which his firm has invested started by focusing on one area of business but ended up focusing on another.

"There are two different kinds of adjustments that we make," Robinson said. "First, there are those ventures that are just trying to do something that is better, quicker, or faster than the processes that they're replacing. In those environments, the pivots are small. They're course corrections."

In other instances, however, leaders need to impose more fundamental changes.

For example, one company in which Robinson invested started with a focus on handwriting recognition. It quickly became clear, however, that the company's product was attracting little consumer interest. The head of engineering suggested a move into a new market, and in response, the company repurposed the algorithms at the core of its business. Today the company focuses on fraud detection and advanced security technology.

Such a major change, said Robinson, required his firm to actively adopt a different perspective and ask itself, "If this were a new company walking in today, would I back this, this way?" And questions like this help companies of all kinds determine when and how much to pivot.

"It's a challenge," Robinson said, "because while you invest in someone's passion for a specific mission, the reality is that most companies start with one specific idea or series of ideas and then adjust. It takes a judgment call to determine: Do we think they've got the ability to repurpose whatever it is they've built today into something else?"

The capacity to pivot, Robinson emphasized, can be the key to innovation and growth.

LEADERSHIP IS MAKING TOUGH DECISIONS

Ultimately, a leader's job is to make tough calls on the basis of sound judgment—hard decisions like when to cut your losses, how to maintain the relationships that can make or break your business, and when you must change course to seize an unanticipated opportunity.

This is the essence of effective leadership, Robinson said. "When there is no easy or obvious answer, when it's a fifty-fifty call, that's when leaders prove their mettle and prove they matter."

LAURA ALBER

Laura Alber is President and CEO of Williams-Sonoma Inc., a premium home-furnishings and gourmet-cookware retailer whose portfolio of successful brands includes Pottery Barn, Pottery Barn Kids, PB Teen, Williams-Sonoma, West Elm, Rejuvenation, and Mark and Graham. A twenty-year veteran of the company, Alber started as a buyer for Pottery Barn and ascended to become president less than a decade later.

Alber is known for her collaborative, creative leadership style. While pregnant with her first child, she and a few fellow mothers-to-be noticed a gap in the market for children's home furnishings and came up with the idea for Pottery Barn Kids. The brand now operates ninety-seven stores around the world, as well as a catalog and e-commerce site. Since Alber took over as CEO, Williams-Sonoma Inc.'s stock has soared, and she was named one of *Fortune's* "2014 Biz People of the Year."

Alber talked about the importance of entrepreneurship and described her approach as a blend of insight and instinct. She shared the best advice she received from the company's founder ("Don't change it. Make it better.") and her own advice for a successful career ("Act like an owner"). Her ingenuity and commitment to excellence can inspire all of us to take initiative and think outside the box.

Williams-Sonoma Inc. has a strong catalog heritage, but you've also achieved great sales through retail stores and online. How do you think about the interplay between those three channels?

They work together really effectively. We just think of them as different ways to connect with the customer. And I think the great thing about our stores is they're so experiential—consumers really connect with products in a unique way. You can smell the Williams-Sonoma store. You look forward to going in and learning something. Then, if you want to just buy something quickly, you can go online. If you'd rather flip through the merchandise, you've got the catalog.

Each channel has its own distinct advantages, and we try to maximize those advantages so it's a rich overall experience. Our best customers tend to shop in all three channels.

In a recent *Harvard Business Review* article, you described how Williams-Sonoma Inc. has worked to blend creative instinct with data-driven analytics to tailor products to your consumers' needs. At The Estée Lauder Companies, we've been on a similar journey over the past few years—striving to build a company that is creativity driven and consumer inspired. How have you adapted your company to integrate and embrace more scientific insights?

Analytics today are amazing. We use sales rates as a barometer of customer acceptance. Then we can break those numbers down by region and other categories to see where people are sensitive to pricing and how placement on the floor and other decisions matter. We've also brought in focus groups to look at our websites and tell us things that aren't as intuitive. You can test subject lines and a lot of other things that may give you a result you wouldn't expect.

It still comes back to the old-school concept of being very close to your customer so you can understand what they're responding to. We take it very personally. If we have a category that's down, we are always self-critical about what's going on there. Where the science is available, we tend to use it and then hold it up against our ideas to see if we're right. So it's one part instinct and one part data. That allows for a good, healthy balance between the intuitive, creative process and the scientific insights that support it.

When you took over as CEO, the company's founder gave you some impressive advice: "Don't change it. Make it better." And that's exactly what you've done at Williams-Sonoma Inc. You've managed to remain loyal to the core identity of the brand while innovating and evolving as the market demands. What's your secret?

For me, that was such an amazing moment because Chuck Williams, our founder, was ninety-four at the time. I had no idea what he was going to tell me, and for him to answer that way was so inspiring to me. I think too many times you come into a leadership position and think you've got to fix all these things, and that means overhauling the whole operation and upending everything. And his advice was, you don't have to approach it that way. You can make it better without tearing everything down and rebuilding it.

It's been a real touchstone for me to respect what's made this company so great: the culture, the history, the quality. And I see new opportunities as just that—as opportunities rather than as criticism of the past. It's more a positive mind-set than anything else, and that helps me lead with a positive energy.

What kind of advice would you give to other leaders in a similar situation, where you've come in to lead a brand with a solid core identity but that may need some polishing and refinement? How would you advise someone to evolve a brand while maintaining its identity and its core values?

I think leaders need a clear vision. Everything starts with a clear vision and a leader who really understands and has a feel for the brand. A lot of that follows from passion. You can study an area and learn a lot about it, but if it's not your passion, you'll probably struggle to connect.

I love being in the home business because it's what I like doing—cooking, entertaining, enjoying our home—even when I'm not working. So it's very personal for me, and I think if it was something I didn't understand, it would be very difficult.

It's so important not only to know the customer, but to be the customer yourself. If you are your own customer, you'll understand intuitively what's attractive, what's going to do well, and what the latest item is that people are looking for. Then you can weigh that against the brand and evolve in a way that honors the traditions and the aesthetic of the company.

Throughout your career, you've spotted unique opportunities and taken advantage of them in ways that others have not. Pottery Barn Kids—which has been enormously successful—was your vision. How did you go about creating the idea, selling the idea, and building the coalition you needed to make it successful?

Pottery Barn Kids was very personal because I was pregnant with my first child, and a few of my colleagues were also pregnant. We had the idea, and we were just obsessed with it. We knew it was going to be huge. At the time, we were criticized for being distracted and not working on the core, so we had to work on it after hours.

We mailed the first catalog, and the response was just incredible. It was the highest dollar per book of anything they'd ever seen. From there, there was talk of opening stores, but we were still getting some resistance. We were so determined that we cleared the parking lot and set up a whole store of product downstairs. And we dragged Howard Lester, our CEO at the time, down there, and I think he was just amazed by the tenacity we all had to put this thing together. He's an entrepreneur, too, and he just said, "All right, all right, all right, let's do this."

So we started opening stores, and it was an immediate success because there was really nothing like it in the market. Today there are a number of competing kids' businesses, but we were really the first to do specialty, high-end kids' home furnishings. And because we were in the life stage, we really understood it.

How important was it to have a CEO who was supportive of your venture and who encouraged entrepreneurship? How do you apply that lesson to your approach as CEO?

There are certain people who you hire and work with who are entrepreneurs by spirit. And you have to have a boss that inspires you to go after those big dreams, even if they're giving you a hard time—which is what Howard did for me. But his hard time made me sharpen every idea. I wrote up a business plan and put the whole thing together before I pitched it.

You can find a lot of people with a lot of good ideas in every company. So as a leader, it's just a matter of listening to them and then prodding the idea further when necessary—or getting out of the way when it's not.

How do you foster that culture of innovation in your organization? How do you spark and sustain it?

The simplest answer is that you just hire great people. It's much less about what I do than about who they are. We seek out people who are always looking for the next opportunity, who have strong personalities, and who are willing to argue. You don't want people who just say, "Okay, yes, ma'am." You want someone who's going to debate and challenge you. I always want strong people around me, and I think we have an incredible team here. It's bigger than any one person. It's everyone really being excellent in their role.

We have a lot of tenured people, but we've also brought in some great new players, too. A lot of them come to us because they like the collaborative environment and the entrepreneurial spirit. They can see that their ideas really come to life here, versus being in a structure that's very top down. So we're always trying wacky stuff, and sometimes it doesn't work. But the wacky stuff pushes you further than you might go otherwise if you just tried to stay in your comfort zone.

Let's talk more about talent. You've been quoted as saying, "Making mistakes on people is one of the biggest mistakes you can make." What do you look for in the people you hire, and how do you avoid making mistakes?

I think when you're looking at talent, results and leadership go hand in hand. I don't think you can have one without the other. So they have to command both the talent and the leadership skills.

It's also important, from a personal standpoint, to like the people you hire. That doesn't mean you have to agree on everything or that you have to be great friends. But you have to enjoy talking and eating dinner and spending time together, because that's all part of the job. So I'm always very careful about who we bring onto the team. We do extensive interviewing in a number of settings—both inside and outside the office—so we can really get to know every candidate.

Talk to us about collaboration. You're known as a great collaborator. And you've built a strong collaborative culture within the Williams-Sonoma Inc. brands. How do you foster effective collaboration across your brands and disciplines?

I think it goes back to how much I respect the people I work with and how talented they are. When you work with great people, you want to hear their point of view. Everyone's united by a passion to win, and they've chosen to come here because they love the businesses we're in.

There's also a lot of resonance with home goods and cooking, and there's a lot to learn. That constant learning also keeps you humble. You may think you're a great chef, but there's always something new to make. This is a very different kind of business, this home business. There are so many different contributing factors, whether it's history, or food trends, or how people are living in their homes. And so just by nature of the business we're in, we're always coming up with ideas and bouncing them off each other.

You mentioned learning. How do you create a learning culture in a company like Williams-Sonoma Inc.? What mechanisms do you have in place to help your team to develop their skills?

We do a few different types of programs that work very well. We have a program called LEAD that I'm really proud of, where we match our director- and vice president-level colleagues with senior executives who serve as their mentors for a year. That has been very effective for us, because it brings people across different brands and different parts of the company together and provides mentorship for up-and-comers in our company.

For me, personally, I tend to get very focused on my job, and I've realized that it's so important for me to stay connected with things that are not always part of my day to day. I read a ton, and I try to go to a few different types of conferences every year and talk to different types of people. I'm trying new things all the time to make sure I don't get too insulated here, because when you've been at a company this long, your biggest fear is that you're going to get complacent in the way you think about things.

Finally, in light of everything we've discussed, if you could share one piece of advice, one kernel of wisdom, for young executives in the first chapters of their careers, what would it be?

Act like an owner. No matter where you are in the hierarchy or in your career. No one wants to hear that you're not sure. You might not be sure, but when you're the owner, you have to be decisive and then stand by your decisions.

> **"Act like an owner. . . . You want to be the person who, instead of complaining about the way things are done, steps forward with new ideas for how to make things better. That's what distinguishes the person who makes a real difference from the person who is just acting like an employee."**
>
> —LAURA ALBER

You want to be the person who, instead of complaining about the way things are done, steps forward with new ideas for how to make things better. That's what distinguishes the person who makes a real difference from the person who is just acting like an employee.

Act like it's your business and you're going to be there forever. Put everything you have into it, and you will get more out than you ever thought possible.

PEOPLE FIRST

LEADERSHIP SPOTLIGHT

Richard D. Parsons

A CONVERSATION WITH

Strauss Zelnick

A CONVERSATION WITH

Michael Berland

PEOPLE FIRST

Leaders are only as good as the people around them. That's why the best leaders surround themselves with good people and empower them to succeed. Great leadership, at its core, is about helping others to be great.

Building a well-balanced team with the right skills and instincts to do the job is even more crucial during uncertain times. When crisis comes, you need people with both strong backbones and level heads to stabilize the organization. That doesn't mean leaders ought to hire only those who share their views. On the contrary, leaders should encourage and seek out team members who are comfortable speaking truth to power. You simply can't succeed by surrounding yourself with yes-men and yes-women who only tell you what you want to hear.

Just as important as a strong team of employees is a collegial, creative, collaborative board of directors. In fact, one of the most delicate personnel operations a leader may face is assembling a board. Which is why a successful board chairman—and I hope to count myself among them—is, above all else, a good casting director.

To date, Dick Parsons ranks among my wisest casting choices. The former Chairman of AOL-Time Warner and Citigroup, who currently chairs the Compensation Committee of The Estée Lauder Companies Board of Directors, understands better than most that—to use his words—"it's all about the people."

By putting people first, Parsons has helped embattled organizations navigate two of the most complex and tenuous corporate crises in recent memory: the failed merger of AOL-Time Warner and the global financial crisis, in which Citigroup played a key role. Through it all,

Parsons projected an unflinching sense of calm, pragmatism, and optimism, the essential qualities every leader needs to reassure and motivate their people in times of crisis.

These are the same qualities demonstrated by Strauss Zelnick and Michael Berland, two leaders who have skillfully guided companies in times of tumult and transition. For Zelnick, it was a string of corporate turnarounds in which his private equity firm worked to earn the trust and loyalty of the beleaguered teams they had inherited. For Berland, it was the challenge of integrating new advanced capabilities into the established culture of the world's largest PR firm.

Each of these leaders offers proof that at the highest ranks of leadership, EQ—emotional intelligence—is as important as IQ. Great leaders must have both and remember that when push comes to shove, people always come first.

RICHARD D. PARSONS

SETTING THE RECORD

Richard D. Parsons is widely regarded as one of the leading corporate-crisis managers in the world of twenty-first-century business. His experiences run deep and wide and include stints leading and advising some of the largest, most noteworthy, and most notorious companies in today's global economy.

During his career, Parsons has served as an aide to US Vice President Nelson Rockefeller, a partner at a major New York law firm, a top executive at a leading regional bank, an adviser to New York Mayor Rudy Giuliani, and as the CEO and Chairman of AOL–Time Warner, and the Chairman of Citigroup. The latter two roles saw Parsons presiding over the ill-fated merger of AOL and Time Warner and steering Citigroup through the 2008–2009 financial crisis. In addition to these roles, Parsons has sat on countless corporate boards, blue-ribbon commissions, and presidential advisory teams.

For all his success, Parsons often jokes, he still "holds the record for losing more money in a quarter and in a year than any other corporate executive in the history of America." All told, he said of the failed AOL–Time Warner merger he oversaw, "I lost $54 billion in one quarter, which translated into about $99 billion for the year. Both records."

The reason Parsons was chosen to preside over one of the biggest mergers in history is simple. He is known for staying cool when temperatures rise—a critical trait for a corporate manager in times of change and challenge.

His key to effective leadership? "Never forget that it's always, always about the people."

MARRYING DIVERGENT CULTURES

The AOL–Time Warner merger has been almost universally described as the worst merger in the history of corporate America.

In 2000, Time Warner was a long-established force in the entertainment industry, a company that encompassed film, music, magazines, and cable divisions. AOL was a flourishing start-up, founded on a commitment to make the Internet "easy, accessible, and usable." Its consumer-oriented mentality made AOL a household name and created the first generation of Internet-savvy users. The name said it all: they were "America Online."

At the time, a merger seemed like an ideal way to create a web-powered, twenty-first-century global media company. With the creative capacities of Time Warner and the ingenuity of AOL, the merger seemed unstoppable.

Until it lost $54 billion in one quarter.

Why? For one, there was the 2001 collapse of the Internet "bubble," but, at an even more basic level, it was a colossal clash of cultures. "The culture of Time Warner was so different and almost anathema to the culture of AOL that it was just impossible to make these things work together," Parsons said.

For instance, when CEO Steve Case presented his idea to make all Time Warner music free to AOL users, the music department was shocked. They had spent their lives working with a business model that was being upended by the (lowercase) new kids on the block.

Ultimately, it wasn't about insufficient intellectual capital or monetary value. The eventual failure of the AOL-Time Warner merger came down to a lack of interpersonal compatibility.

"Horizontal mergers—mergers of companies in the same line of business—work," Parsons said. "Vertical mergers, where you take different businesses, organized around different kinds of skill sets, and stack them one on top of the other—they're much more difficult."

And when two merging companies share no chemistry from the C-suite to the sales team, success is more challenging. "The importance of culture is not to be underestimated," Parsons said. "Culture is an enormously important thing."

TWO CATEGORIES OF MANAGERS: CRISIS STATE AND STEADY STATE

According to Parsons, leadership is about skills in context, not skills in isolation—and not all skills are well suited to every context.

After seeing AOL-Time Warner through the roughest turbulence of its transition, Parsons knew it was time to hand over the reins.

"When you inherit an organization that's in crisis," he explained, "it needs focus and intensity around very select things, because survival is at stake. Once you get those things fixed, then you need focus and attention on a whole number of things to keep the organization moving forward—and that's never been my core competency."

How do effective managers right a ship's course? Parsons identified several essential actions: Getting people focused on their jobs, not the drama around them. Stopping the bleeding—whether by stabilizing cash flow or minimizing turnover. And, most importantly, ensuring that management has the credibility to manage.

"When I became CEO of AOL-Time Warner, I took the two guys who ran our most successful divisions and I made them co-COOs of the company," Parsons recalled.

"Right away, everybody said, 'This guy must be serious. This must really be about the best interests of the company, not the personal interests of the guy in charge.' Organizations almost always know who's the real deal and who isn't."

Crisis-time leadership, Parsons said, is a bit like piloting the *Titanic*. "When you hit the iceberg, you need everyone to get down there and fix the hole. The morning's breakfast menu, the next day's activities, or the next port of call—they all become irrelevant in the face of a clear objective."

Fundamentally, Parsons said of his time at the helm of AOL-Time Warner, "effective leaders do two things really well: They define reality—identifying 'What do we have to do to be successful?' And then they give hope—reassuring that 'Hey, we can do this.'"

THE ROLE OF THE BOARD: MANAGING THE MANAGERS

The lessons Parsons learned during the AOL-Time Warner merger proved invaluable when Parsons took on his next challenge: stewarding Citigroup through the financial crisis. Once again, Parsons said, the most important thing he did was recognize that the regulators, shareholders, and stakeholders involved weren't inanimate objects; they were people.

This insight was especially crucial as Parsons led Citigroup's board of directors. For several years before the financial crisis, Citi and many of its peer institutions had avoided including bankers on their boards of directors. Why? "Because if you're the management, you don't want somebody telling you how to do your business," said Parsons.

Ultimately, Parsons said, this custom was one of the factors that contributed to the financial crisis. Few members of Citigroup's board had any experience or expertise in banking, and as a result, they failed to adequately probe the bank's management about the risky behavior several of its operating divisions were engaged in.

And so, as part of Citigroup's response to the meltdown, Citi—and others—agreed to replace several members of its governing body.

It was a delicate balancing act. Citigroup needed a board with the right mix of people to help guide the company, but it also needed to preserve the relationships, credibility, and institutional knowledge that would allow it to govern effectively.

In restructuring the board, Parsons sought out high-quality people who knew the business and could help the board ask the right questions and effectively manage—and monitor—the managers.

It's essential to have a governing body with the right mix of experience and expertise, skills and strengths, Parsons said.

"As board members, we can't manage the business, but with the right team working together, we can establish and then measure key metrics and hold management accountable. That's what gave us, and the regulators, confidence. That's the lesson we learned from 2008."

IT'S ALL ABOUT THE PEOPLE

Ultimately, said Parsons, you can't create a structure that is going to solve your problem. "That's the job of a leader. Leaders figure out, what do I have to do to get my people from where they are as a group to where I need them to be?"

Regardless of the situation, leaders must communicate well, earn trust, and inspire confidence. In the midst of crisis, Parsons said, "good leaders get people to believe in them; great leaders get people to believe in themselves."

"If you can convince a room full of people, or an auditorium full of people, or a stadium full of people, or a country full of people that they have it within their power to execute the plan that you have collectively embraced, they can make it happen," Parsons said. "And that is a powerful thing."

STRAUSS ZELNICK

S trauss Zelnick has found success in nearly every segment of the entertainment industry. After serving as head of the music giant BMG Entertainment, film studio 20th Century Fox, and video game developer Crystal Dynamics, Zelnick founded his own company, ZelnickMedia, in 2001. ZelnickMedia is a private equity firm with investments in numerous media enterprises, including Take-Two Interactive Software, the video game developer best known for its blockbuster *Grand Theft Auto* series.

Zelnick is a specialist in the art of the turnaround, shepherding faltering companies back to profitability and transforming them into hit machines. He took the reins at Take-Two with the company's leadership in turmoil and has successfully reestablished, grown, and diversified the brand, producing a flurry of best-selling titles.

In a candid conversation, Zelnick shared his rules for a successful turnaround (he has a 100 percent success rate) and explained why he considers lying the only unforgivable sin in business. He discussed his approach to keeping his cool in a crisis and the philosophy of servant leadership that he brings to each of his companies. His humility, insight, and propensity for kindness can serve all of us as we develop as leaders, colleagues, and professionals.

You're known for your ability to turn around faltering companies. Walk us through your process. Where do you begin?

The first rule is an obvious one: you have to choose the right turnaround. The fact is, certain things can't be turned around, and if anyone thinks their executive skills are going to trump the facts, it's nonsense. Good decision making is as important as good management when it comes to leadership, and one of the reasons we have a 100 percent success rate in turnarounds is that we were selective in the first place.

All of our businesses have to meet certain criteria before we take them on as a turnaround. First and foremost, we have to like the sector, because you can turn around a company, but you can't turn around a sector. We also need to have a mathematical bridge to profitability. We don't want to bet that we're geniuses who can increase revenue. We want to be able to take a company exactly as we find it and, through cost reduction, generate profitability.

The second rule is, you need a quality balance sheet. If you take over an overleveraged enterprise, you're just going to find yourself back in a problem because, among other things, you can't make good decisions when you're constantly dealing with a bad balance sheet.

The third rule is, you have to be the first team in. Again, that falls into the category of not being overly excited about your own skill set. If another team has gone in and failed, you need to understand what happened and why. By the time you go in, all the low-hanging fruit will have been picked, and the team will already be exhausted. They're not going to be eager to follow another leadership team that's making them the same promises the last one couldn't deliver. So we never do a turnaround if we're the second team in.

Once you've selected your turnaround, what are the next steps?

The first order of business is relatively straightforward. We put together a list of projects. Some people call it a hundred-day plan. Then we gather the team we have together.

We never go in guns blazing, because we don't know anything. So even though the people that are there are probably substandard by definition, they're the team we've got. So we work with them, we get to know them, and we always tell them the truth.

The first day, I do a town hall meeting with the entire staff, even if it's a big company, and say, "Look, I will never lie to you. I'll tell you the truth. We've never failed to do a turnaround. We have a lot of confidence here. I cannot promise you you'll have your jobs when we're through our initial process, but I can promise you that you'll be in a lot better shape if you come together with us and try to do well than if you don't. And you can ask me any question, and I'll answer it honestly."

Then we take our list of projects and roll up our sleeves and do the hard work. It starts with cost reduction, and then we get into revenue enhancement and business-model changes. That's our basic operating model. All of our employees have milestones against which we check progress weekly, and we keep doing that until all our initial tasks are completed.

How do you keep everyone focused on the goals and moving in the same direction?

One of the most important things we do is make sure incentives are completely aligned among the employees and the shareholders. We do that by paying people fair, median, base compensation and making bonus compensation formulaic and related to achieving or exceeding annual financial targets. That's true top to bottom, from the highly influential senior executive all the way down to the controller who has no influence over revenues and profits.

The effect of that is powerful. Everyone pulls in the same direction. Everyone understands that if you're not pulling in the same direction, you're not going to get paid.

It also eliminates a lot of the politics. If you want to create an apolitical atmosphere, making all compensation formulaic is a good place to start. I always tell my employees, "You are not going to get paid more for smiling at me in the hallway, or saying nice things to me, or telling me what you think I want to hear. And that goes both ways. If you tell me something I don't want to hear or pound on the table, you're not going to get paid less."

Do you have any other hard and fast rules for your turnarounds?

We're not rule based, but we can't make good decisions on bad information. So I tell my employees on day one, "We only have one rule, and that's if you lie to us, we will fire you summarily."

And we mean it. It's been tested, and usually in a very sad way, where someone who's otherwise competent screws up, and we actually fire him or her. But we have to do it. We can't do anything well if we don't have trustworthy information.

We have a multibillion-dollar enterprise, and in the fourteen years that we've been in business, we've never been surprised. We've had plenty of things go against us, but we've been able to optimize the bulk of our decisions.

Talk to us about your turnaround of Take-Two. You looked at it and saw the sector was good, the bones of the company were good, but it hadn't been managed properly. How did you transform the company, particularly from a management perspective, into the profitable brand it is today?

When we showed up at Take-Two, it was not a pretty scene. The chairman had just been indicted for backdating stock options. The CFO was under investigation by the SEC. The company was under investigation by the SEC, the New York DA's office, and the IRS. Costs were too high, and they didn't have much capital. And everyone on the creative team—which is really the heart and soul of the company—was ready to jump ship.

So what did we do? We embarked on a meaningful cost-reduction plan and, in six months, cut $40 million out of operating costs. We shored up their credit line. I personally met with the New York DA's office, the IRS, and the SEC, told them about our team's track record, and assured them I had never had any issues with compliance and didn't intend to. We got all those problems settled quickly with very low costs.

How did you persuade the creative team to stay on with you? What did you have to do to build a rapport and earn their trust?

I did it in two ways, and because I'm in a creative business, this leadership has a slightly different twist.

The first was sitting down face to face with people and pitching them directly. I went to many of our creative heads—who made it clear they were set on leaving—and I said, "I'm not going to try to convince you to stay. But do me one favor. Give me three months. If at the end of three months you want to go, you'll go with my blessing." Most of them said okay, and many of them, after seeing what we had to offer, ultimately decided to stay.

The second way I earned trust was by adding value as a leader. We had a situation early on where a major film studio was threatening to use our IP without purchasing the rights. I saw it as a test of my legitimacy because the prior CEO and management team were incapable of solving problems. They would just litigate everything. I called the head of production, with whom I had a personal relationship, and managed to convince him that moving forward with this project would be a bad move for the studio. It was something only I could have done

> "My view of being a leader is you solve problems for your team. You serve at your team's pleasure."
>
> —STRAUSS ZELNICK

because of my prior experience in the industry and the relationships I had built.

That episode sent an important message to our creative team about our intention to support them and to go to bat for them. The leadership of the company had never solved a problem for this group before. Their view of being a leader was, "We sit in the corner office and tell you what to do now and then." My view of being a leader is you solve problems for your team. You serve at your team's pleasure.

> "It's our job to serve the team and help them do their jobs better."
>
> —STRAUSS ZELNICK

Can you elaborate on that? What does it mean to "serve at your team's pleasure"?

I always tell my leadership team, it's our job as corporate—since we don't make anything, we don't manufacture anything, we don't create any value—it's our job to serve the team and help them do their jobs better. If we're on the phone or an e-mail exchange with someone who works at one of our companies, we should be adding value in that exchange. If we're not adding value in the exchange, don't have the exchange, because we serve at their pleasure.

You mentioned you have a 100 percent success rate in your turn-arounds, but surely you've faced a few crises along the way. How do you approach leadership during a crisis? What lessons have you learned in the course of your career that have helped you manage these situations more effectively?

I have two rules for leadership in a crisis. The first is don't raise your voice, and the second is don't panic. In any crisis situation, I think it helps to have lived for a while. This is where there is some correlation between age and leadership, because life experiences give you lessons to draw from and help to put things into perspective.

I dealt with a crisis on our very first turnaround. It was a public Japanese company, and we'd only owned it for nine months. I had hired a CEO who'd worked for me before, a Japanese national, and I was the company chairman.

We knew this CEO had been battling cancer, but we were told he was okay when we hired him. The last taboo in Japan is illness—people don't talk about it—so we could never ask him directly. Nine months in, he died suddenly.

I got a call in the middle of the night, and I cancelled my vacation and flew to Japan. We found out quickly that during the previous month and a half, he had misled us with regard to the company's numbers because he'd known he was dying and didn't want to go out with bad information. So I met with the banks and calmed them down. I met with the staff and calmed them down. I named myself CEO and said I would run the company. We had to disclose the new numbers to the public markets, and the stock tanked. We had just raised money in secondary, so everyone was very upset with me.

I remember getting a call from an investor, and he's screaming at me in the phone, "This is a disaster, this is a disaster." And I said, "Stop. You know what a disaster is? A disaster is a sick child. This is business. And I'm really sorry that this is the situation. I'm doing the very best I can with it. But you know what? If it goes against me, it's still just business. It'll be okay."

That approach has always served me and helped me resolve problems more effectively in the midst of a crisis. I was still worried, but I took a step back, I made a plan, and six months later we succeeded in turning around the business. The lesson I learned, which I was able to apply to subsequent turnarounds, is if you stay calm and focused, if you have a plan, and if you recognize that even if the plan fails you will still go on, you can get through nearly anything.

If you could share one or two key pieces of advice for future leaders who are just starting the first chapter of their careers, what would they be?

I've found that the best advice I've received has inevitably fallen into three categories.

The first is get up early, stay late, and work hard. That seems sort of tautological, but the truth is that when you are starting out, nothing distinguishes you from your peers. You all have about the same education. You all look good. You're all capable and sensible. So the only thing that's really going to distinguish you early on is willingness to work hard. There's really no substitute for hard work.

The second piece of advice is listen. Listen deeply and with empathy. You never know what you might learn, and showing people that respect and kindness can be very powerful as well.

The third piece of advice is never compromise your integrity. It's all you have.

I've been far from perfect in my career, but this advice has always served me extraordinarily well.

MICHAEL BERLAND

Michael Berland is the CEO of Edelman Berland, the strategic insights, analytics, and research arm of Edelman PR, the world's largest PR firm. He is the former president of the market research and political communications firm Penn Schoen Berland and is an internationally renowned consultant.

Berland has advised on the campaigns of New York City Mayor Michael Bloomberg and on Hillary Clinton's campaigns for US Senate and President. He is an expert pollster and an industry leader in the use of data for targeted communication.

Berland partnered with Richard Edelman in 2012 and has led the company's charge to integrate real-time research and insights into its PR strategy and programs. As CEO of Edelman Berland, Berland works with some of the world's largest companies and nonprofits, as well as leaders in the political, entertainment, and sports industries.

The author of a book on leadership and success, Berland shared his take on the leadership styles and traits that define some of the world's most respected leaders. The PR expert talked about the importance of introspection ("There's a class that they don't teach at college that should be called Introspection 101") and offered his quick and dirty guide to crisis management ("Go to rehab as quickly as possible").

In a 24/7 world, Berland's advice can help all of us stay ahead of the curve and manage the unexpected with grace.

**Your book *What Makes You Tick?* identifies four "success arche-
types" that describe most successful leaders: Natural-Born Leaders,
Visionaries, Independence Seekers, and Do-Gooders. I was honored
to be listed in the Visionaries category, but the point of the book is
that there are many different paths to and personalities suited for
success. Can you tell us a bit about each category?**

With all the leaders I interviewed, I saw you could look back to
moments in their lives and see the ingredients for success in their DNA.
What I found was that each leadership style brings together a different
mix of motivations and styles.

Natural-Born Leaders gravitate toward positions of leadership.
They seek to inspire others and are driven to help them succeed. They
are eager to climb as high as possible and be recognized faster and
younger than anyone else.

Visionaries are single minded and inventive. They see something—a product, a service, a process—and want to improve it. If it
ain't broke, they fix it anyway. They create new paradigms in our lives,
and their ideas become the touchstones for everyone who follows them.
Failures are just part of the process; they learn and move on.

Independence Seekers are goal oriented. They seek out the challenges they find intellectually interesting or emotionally gratifying,
accomplish them, and move on to the next venture. Their key goal is
personal independence—intellectual and financial. Money is important for the freedom it brings, not for the yachts it buys.

Do-Gooders find fulfillment in helping others. They are willing to
make personal sacrifices for the greater good, and their style is focused
on personal contact and connection. They see their goals and the goals
of their organization as intertwined with the progress of the people
around them.

Which one describes you?

I am definitely an Independence Seeker—I have always loved taking on new kinds of tasks and new challenges. In my professional career, I began by building a successful business where we brought the lessons from the campaign trail to the boardroom, then sold the company to the WPP Group, and have now started Edelman Berland to reinvent and reimagine the role of research within the communications world. I am always restless to move to the next stage. I have loved transforming the industry I started in twenty-five years ago—from episodic to continuous, anonymous to social, evaluating to informing communications.

Once you've discovered your archetype, how do you use that information to lead more effectively?

Using your archetype means putting yourself in situations where you can leverage your strengths to be successful. You have to understand what it is that motivates you and then use that knowledge to drive your performance. As a leader, knowing your archetype also helps you determine where you are strongest and where you might benefit from additional backup. For example, if you are a Visionary, you may look to bring more Independence Seekers onto your team to tackle short-term goals while you manage the company's long-term vision. Everyone doesn't need to be great at everything. But great organizations put the right people in the right positions for success.

What do you do when you have an executive who is successful in their role—because the responsibilities match their natural tendencies— and they come to you seeking to apply for a different job that you know won't be a good fit?

That's the recurring pattern—everybody gravitates towards their weaknesses. Very few people deep dive into their strengths. They always want to solve for their weaknesses. So the managers want to be sales. The sales want to be managers. The analysts want to be writers.

We can only excel at so many things, so it's illogical for people to chase their weaknesses. And as a manager, I spend a lot of my time counseling people against doing the illogical, because it always seems very logical to them. So I try to probe their motivations a little deeper, and I remind them that as a team, we're going to perform best when everyone is playing to their strengths.

> "As a team, we're going to perform best when everyone is playing to their strengths."
>
> —MICHAEL BERLAND

You've spoken about the importance of introspection and of knowing your own passions, strengths, and weaknesses. What are some of the key questions every young leader should ask him- or herself?

There's a class that they don't teach at college that should be called Introspection 101. It would serve people incredibly well. Before they ever embark on their careers, they should have the option to spend a semester understanding themselves. This could be as simple as having the opportunity to take an internship rotation in different industries, or merely having an elective class to take something that just sounds interesting to them—separate from their core studies. It would put young people on such a nice trajectory into the future rather than getting sidetracked by what they think they should do.

The real key is avoiding the "I should" thinking. Look over everything you've done—school, sports, work, volunteering. What are you good at? What do you really enjoy doing? I'm not saying money isn't important, but if what you're doing doesn't fit who you are, you won't make it in the long haul anyway. If every kid could answer those few questions about themselves, they would know what to study, what to dive deep into, and what to avoid.

How did you figure out your calling?

Completely by accident. I had a seminal moment early in my life when I was interested in politics. I ran for class president twice in high school. One time I lost by two votes, and the next year I lost again to a classmate who I felt was not equipped for the job. I decided in that moment that I no longer wanted to be the king. I wanted to be the king-maker. I realized I wanted to be an adviser, and in fact, I wrote my college application essay—which I didn't realize was controversial at the time—on how I could have kept Richard Nixon from having to resign.

Once I knew what I wanted to do, I pursued an internship in New York working with Penn + Schoen. I quickly found myself dealing with important people from huge international corporations to candidates running for office, and I loved it. I realized this was not a summer job; it was my calling. If you can find what you love doing—what you are passionate about—you can build a fulfilling life and a lifelong career.

You began at Penn + Schoen as a summer intern during college and worked your way up to partner, CEO, and president, with your name on the door. How have Mark Penn's and Doug Schoen's leadership styles influenced yours?

Mark Penn and Doug Schoen were incredibly important influences on me when I first began working. They were very different personality types, but I was able to learn key lessons from each of them.

Penn taught me to be creative and challenge the conventional wisdom. Never take the obvious answer. He also taught me to believe in technology and its power. He was one of those guys who was building computers from kits in the seventies like Bill Gates and Steve Wozniak.

But Penn was more comfortable reading poll numbers about people than he was actually talking to people.

Schoen was the opposite. He was incredibly intuitive and gregarious, with a photographic memory—a true intellectual. He taught me this great lesson of the charm and the chum. He said, "Mike, all relationships are either charm relationships or chum relationships. A chum is a real friend who you get along with and who will take your advice freely. A charm is someone who you're never going to be friends with but who you have to endear yourself to up to the level where you've earned their trust and respect." And that really stuck with me—the charm and the chum. It helped me interact with all of my clients and understand what kind of relationship to pursue in each individual case—because so much of my job is not about what I say, but how it's received and acted upon.

After twenty-five years at Penn Schoen Berland, you joined Edelman in 2012 to head Edelman Berland, the firm's new insights and analytics unit. How did you build your own culture at Edelman Berland while maintaining a connection to the established Edelman brand?

My challenge at Edelman is about cultural transformation. I've been on a two-year journey to transform the PR industry, which was built entirely on instinct, into a business that is grounded in data-driven insights and measurable results. So much of my job is not actually working with clients—who already get it—but working internally to change a culture and demonstrate how research and insights can grow a business and transform a company.

We have buy-in from senior leadership, who have helped spread our mandate, but winning over the rank and file of the five thousand people who are under the top ten is actually quite challenging, and we spend a lot of time working on educating and influencing that group. I've had incredible support in this transformation to align incentives so that our employees can benefit from the research that they sell. Yet we (Edel-man Berland) have to continuously demonstrate how this expertise can actually help them (Edelman) win new business and grow deeper engagements with our potential and existing clients. We have had to change the business model. It's been very challenging and eye-opening for the older, more experienced PR people who are used to operating in a completely different paradigm—one where they led and won with instinct—as we shift to predicting outcomes and measuring results.

You've been working in the communications world for more than two decades, during which time the Internet and social media have completely transformed the way we communicate. How did you adapt your company to so much change?

Today we, and all of our clients, live in a 24/7 world. There is no more news cycle. Anything can happen anywhere at any moment and can impact your business, your image, and your reputation. So we have to be all-knowing and ready to jump at any second.

My staff monitors social media news feeds all day long, and we have sophisticated alerts that keep us one step ahead of what's going on. We've developed a new dashboard tool that allows us to monitor all the news from both social and traditional outlets. It's not just about what happens in the client's home territory—events halfway around the world can have just as great an impact on image and perceptions.

Speaking of adaptability, you're in a client-based business, advising clients on the trends of the future. How do you encourage them to adapt their forward-looking strategies to the reality as you see it?

Instinct is still incredibly valuable, but it has to be married with data-driven insights. That's what I did as a pollster and still do today, except now companies like Facebook have analytic capabilities that would blow your mind. And so the world has actually moved in my direction. I'll rarely make a point without data to back it up.

One component of PR that hasn't changed is crisis management. You've advised numerous leaders on what and how to communicate during a crisis. Can you share some of those lessons with us? What should leaders say and do, and what common mistakes should they avoid making?

I'll give you the quick and dirty guide. It's actually a four-step process.

Step one: understand the extent of the problem. BP's biggest problem in the aftermath of the oil spill wasn't the oil. It was that they didn't know the extent of the damage. They made blunder after blunder trying to minimize the problem without actually knowing how big it was, and they ended up looking like they were lying or covering up.

Step two: acknowledge the problem. Denial just delays the inevitable and makes the eventual revelation even more damaging. You can't talk your way out of a crisis, but you will earn respect for transparency and for addressing it head-on.

Step three: put forward a clear and demonstrable solution. This one is self-explanatory.

Step four: go to rehab. This means taking action that restores confidence and assures the public that it will never happen again. The key in any crisis is to go to rehab as quickly as possible.

If you ignore these four steps, you won't get away with it. The problem will come back and continue to hurt you. With the Internet, crises are more prevalent and more public than ever before, and companies need to be even more proactive in responding to and handling them.

Finally, in light of everything we've discussed, if you could share one piece of advice—one kernel of wisdom—to young leaders in the first few chapters of their careers, what would it be?

I think the best piece of advice I've received was from Michael Bloomberg, who always said, "Make a promise, keep a promise." It's so simple and yet so profound. I repeat it to myself and to everybody who works with me. If you say you're going to do it, just do it, and don't find reasons not to.

LEADERSHIP IN ACTION

WILLIAM P. LAUDER

INTERVIEW BY MICHAEL USEEM, PH.D.

In the making of this book, William P. Lauder interviewed a number of prominent executives and decision makers. But there was one visionary leader he could not interview: himself. Having worked so closely with William and the Company, I know that he, too, has extensive experience making tough decisions in the leadership chair—and that the wisdom he has gained in the process is second to none. Indeed, Fabrizio Freda has often credited William with providing some of the best advice he's received in his career, sharing that he "relies on William's knowledge, experience, and judgment on a daily basis."

In this final chapter, I turn the tables on William so you can follow his leadership journey—in his own words—from the Wharton classroom to The Estée Lauder Companies C-suite.

When you were growing up, did you always envision yourself going into the family business?

I have been around the business my whole life, so I like to say that I joined the Company fifty-four years ago—but I've only been paid for it for the last twenty-nine years.

Honestly, I did not always see myself becoming the head of the Company. Like most children who imagine what they'll be when they grow up, I didn't necessarily want to follow in my parents' footsteps. In fact, I wanted to be a professional baseball player, or a competitive skier, or an airline pilot, depending on when you asked me.

I may have picked something up from the conversation at the dinner table, but I eventually started to realize that I could be pretty good at this. And so, at some point, I decided that getting involved in the family company was something that I wanted to pursue.

How did you begin your career?

After I graduated from Wharton in 1983, my first job was working for Donald Regan, who was the United States Secretary of the Treasury under President Ronald Reagan.

I thought that was fascinating—very heady. I had an incredible amount of responsibility for someone my age, which is a common thing in government and politics. I was still in my twenties, and I was advising senior people who had been appointed or elected.

I knew that I didn't plan to spend my career in the government, though, and I needed to gain some business experience. I wanted to find an environment where I could succeed on my own, not because my dad was the boss, which is why I decided to join Macy's.

I completed the Macy's executive-training program in New York City and went on to become associate merchandising manager of the New York Division. Working at Macy's for three years, I was able to develop an understanding of how one of our key customers operates. Then, after I spent about a year in Dallas opening a new store, I decided to move back to New York and join The Estée Lauder Companies.

What lessons did you learn during those early years that have stuck with you?

Early on, when I was working for Secretary Regan, I was lucky enough to have a little one-on-one time with him, and he gave me some advice. Now here is an accomplished leader, who had been the chief executive of Merrill Lynch, had been a Marine colonel, and was leading this huge organization—the US Treasury—so, of course, I was going to listen.

"If you're not in control of your calendar, you're not in control of your life," he told me. "You should always be in control of your calendar."

I've made that a mantra for my life. Now, there are some things that you can't necessarily change, like what time a flight takes off. But what I mean by control, to the extent that it's possible, is saying, "I'm doing what I'm doing when I'm doing it because I choose to, because this is important to me." If you can stay in control of your time, you will become a more effective manager and leader.

Another lesson I learned is that you never know when opportunity will knock, but it will find you if you're open to it. In my case, after I had been at Macy's for a couple of years, Rose Marie Bravo—then a Macy's executive and my mentor—called me into her office and said, "I want you to move to Dallas and open a new store for us."

I'd lived in Philadelphia and Washington—even France—but I'm a New Yorker through and through. I never imagined that I would live in Texas.

So, I went from jamming myself into the subway at Seventy-Second Street and Broadway to driving down the highway to a store on the edge of Dallas. I wouldn't trade the experience for anything, because I learned so much and gained an appreciation for a different part of American culture. If you had asked me when I started, though, whether my career trajectory would take me to Texas, the answer would have been "no way."

All these years later, I still draw on the lessons I learned from my time in Dallas. And Rose Marie, the leader who challenged me to expand my horizons, remains a mentor and close friend, as well as a valued member of The Estée Lauder Companies Board of Directors.

Can you describe the transition to working for The Estée Lauder Companies?

When you're a member of the family in a family business, you have to work twice as hard for half the credit because everyone is looking at you and thinking that you didn't get here because of what you were able to accomplish. You're constantly trying to prove your ability—not necessarily in competition with others, but by demonstrating how you can make a difference.

I started out at The Estée Lauder Companies as a regional brand manager, so it was an area where I had some experience and expertise, at a relatively low level. There were about thirty others just like me in this one division of the Company, and my goal was to distinguish myself from my peers. Two years later, I was promoted to a different brand with a broader scope of responsibility. Again I had the same approach and tried to demonstrate my ability.

The most significant experience came when I had the opportunity to really be an entrepreneur inside the Company. In 1990, I led the team that launched our Origins brand. As a thirty-year-old, it was one of the biggest challenges I'd faced in my life. It was all-consuming, but it was an incredibly stimulating experience to put together a team, create a business model, and build a brand from scratch.

Operating inside the larger organization, we had something of a safety net below us, which allowed me to be more entrepreneurial and break some of the rules that typically applied in the industry. The people with whom I worked were fabulous and energetic, and I learned a great deal about what it takes to be an effective manager and leader.

Ultimately, we were very successful, and I used that success as a platform to drive internal change in our Company.

What, specifically, made Origins different?

As a reformed retailer myself, having worked at Macy's, I recognized the strengths and weaknesses of our department store partners. So after launching Origins in department stores, I decided that we should open our own retail stores.

At the time, in 1990, that was heresy in our industry, and it was heresy inside our Company. I got a lot of pushback—from senior leaders and from everyone who believed that their careers depended on selling to the department stores. My mission was to prove that a retail store strategy could succeed. And I was willing to take the heat because I knew that it was the right thing to do for the brand and for our Company. Today, our Company operates more than a thousand retail stores globally, and in FY 2014, we became our own largest customer. We sell more to the consumer directly through our own freestanding stores and e-commerce sites and platforms than we do through any single retail partner.

Looking back, it's clear that controlling your own retail stores allows you to better control your brand identity and express your brand equity. It wasn't apparent to everyone at the time, though, and I was probably in a better position to try it, to push us, because of my last name. The worst thing that could have happened was that I could fail, but I didn't really worry about that. I was pretty confident that this was the right decision for us at that time, and if you're not willing to try and fail, you'll never know whether you can succeed.

Then, in the late 1990s, everything was *Internet, Internet, Internet.* The Internet was going to kill the newspaper. The Internet was going to kill the store. The Internet was going to make everyone stay home all the time and have everything delivered to them. If you lived in the ancient world of bricks and mortar, you were doomed.

In the retail industry, especially, the sky was falling. We were told that there was a finite amount of consumption, so more buying online meant less buying in stores. Instead of following the traditional ortho-doxy, we decided to develop an online presence and communicate with consumers. That was controversial, but again I felt this was the right decision for our Company. Two years later, when we turned on our first e-commerce site, it was even more controversial because our retail part-ners perceived it as a threat to their business. We had to work very hard to convince them that it wasn't.

We understand now that our online presence enhances our overall business. We know that the multichannel consumer who shops online and in-store, whether at our own retail stores or department stores, is a far more valuable customer, who spends more on our brands than the consumer who shops exclusively online or in-store. And we also know that the link with the highest click rates on each of our brand websites is always the store locator. So as good as the business of e-commerce may be, there are still many, many consumers who want to know where they can see, touch, feel, and smell the product before they buy it.

After your success with Origins, did you feel that you were prepared to become CEO of the entire Company?

Once I successfully established the Origins brand, I started to receive more leadership opportunities. In the mid-1990s, ELC acquired two brands, MAC and Bobbi Brown. I oversaw their management, while continuing to lead Origins. I then led the worldwide business at Clinique. I was named Chief Operating Officer in 2003 and became Chief Executive Officer in 2004.

I was only the third CEO in our Company's history. The first was my father, Leonard A. Lauder. His successor was Fred Langhammer, who's not part of the family but who had spent his career in our Company. My view was that I didn't get the job because of my name. It was important that I earned it and proved myself with the success that I had.

It's fascinating to see the difference between your impression of leaders when you're young and when, all of a sudden, you grow up and are one of them. When I was nine years old at sleepaway camp, the senior campers were giants—they were as tall as trees to me. Not so many years later, I was one of them and thought, "I'm not really as big as they were back then." But I was.

I use that as an example to say, when you are starting out in your career, you may be intimidated by the senior executives. But when you reach that level of leadership, you realize that you still put your shoes on one foot at a time like everybody else. And you still have as much to learn as anyone, even if you face different challenges day in and day out.

You were the CEO for five years before you hired Fabrizio Freda and became executive chairman. Was that a difficult decision?

It really wasn't a difficult decision for me. The reality was I didn't have the time to accomplish everything I wanted to accomplish from a leadership standpoint as long as I was doing it alone. Our Company was doing well, but to prepare for the future, I believed we needed to make some fundamental changes to the ways we were doing business.

As you might imagine, it's very difficult to get an organization to agree to big changes—particularly when things are going well. But I felt very strongly that if we didn't change, there was a time in the not too distant future when things would not be going as well. So first I had to work with our Board to get consensus around the changes I believed were necessary, and then I started looking for someone who could be my partner and a catalyst and an agent for change.

There were members of my team who resisted the change and especially resisted the idea of bringing someone in from outside to lead the Company. Some of them ended up leaving as a result. But that was something I had to accept, because I knew this was the direction we needed to go, and at the end of the day, if they were not willing to be part of the change, they were going to be an obstacle to it.

So we started the search, and as luck would have it, the very first candidate I met was Fabrizio Freda. He had me at a little more than hello, and I saw the potential for a great partnership right away. I told him how I saw the industry shifting and the potential I saw for our Company to evolve, and he seemed to share my vision. Just as importantly, his personality fit, and I felt very comfortable working with him. His background is different than mine, so we both have our lanes of expertise and competence, and then we have areas where we know we need to come together.

It was about a six-month courting process, and during that time we spent a lot of time talking and making sure that we were on the same page about what we needed to accomplish. I managed to convince him both to leave his longtime employer, Procter & Gamble, and to move his family from tranquil, historic Rome to hectic New York to work for our Company. He joined as COO for about fifteen months, at which point I was confident in the decision to make him CEO and move myself to Executive Chairman.

We've had a successful partnership ever since. We work very well together, mainly because we took the time early on to get on the same page about our shared mission and agreed that if we led that mission together, we could get our organization there.

How did your decision to hire a new CEO reflect the way you think about leadership in general?

As a leader, it's extraordinarily important to surround yourself with people in whom you have total confidence—both in their ability and their willingness to be totally honest in private about their concerns and what they need to be successful.

But you can't do everything by yourself, especially in a large organization. I think good leaders have the humility to understand that.

I love to use baseball as an analogy. There are nine players on the field, each with a different role and skill set. When the ball is hit to the third baseman, his job is not to run all the way to first base to tag the runner. He is going to throw the ball to the first baseman, whose job is to catch the ball. Any great organization is a team of highly skilled people who work well together, respect each other, and understand their individual responsibilities.

At the end of the day, a big part of leadership is making sure that everybody is in the right place at the right time to achieve the objective—and creating an environment that allows others to thrive.

What else have you learned about how to create that environment?

The more you give of your time, and the more you teach people that you value and trust them, the more willing they are to stretch beyond what they thought they were capable of to achieve something.

To me, one of the most important elements of leadership is presence. As you grow in your leadership, you come to realize that it's not just about being on the phone and participating in a conference call; it's about physically showing up and making an effort that makes people understand that they are important.

I've always been told from people who met President Bill Clinton only once that he made them feel like they were the only person who mattered. That was one of the defining characteristics of his ability as a leader—he made everyone he met feel like he cared about them.

There are gestures that may appear to be small gestures, but in the long run make a real difference. For example, I always make it a point during the holiday season to visit our key stores, particularly in New York City, where people are working all day and all night, often standing on their feet. And I just go to say, "Thank you. How are you? I'm thinking about you."

Ultimately, the success of the organization is dependent on the satisfaction of our employees. And I want our employees to take pride in everything we stand for as a company. That means not only having success from a business standpoint, but also having a value system that makes people happy to come to work every day.

What's different about leading a family company versus a nonfamily company?

Leading a family company and being a member of that family is both a pressure and privilege.

In many ways the stakes are higher in a family company because it's your name on the brand and on the door and you can't just walk away if things go south. You are the keeper of the culture—it's your responsibility to honor and respect the past without letting it hold the company back from its future potential. You also have to balance the interests of other family members who may have strong opinions and who feel a similar sense of investment and stake in the future of the company. When I was CEO, our largest shareholders shared my last name and had my home phone number—and weren't afraid to use it.

At the same time, there is a real advantage to leading a company that is focused on longevity and on generating long-term value. When most analysts say "long-term," they mean three months from now. When most companies create a long-term strategy, they are looking at the next three years. Our Company has a Ten-Year Strategic Compass process that allows us to look ahead and chart our future as the leader in our industry. We practice what I call "patient capitalism"—as a family company, we have a higher tolerance for long-term investments that yield greater returns five, ten, fifteen years into the future.

How did The Estée Lauder Companies become the global leader in prestige beauty?

On a basic strategic level, we were one of the first companies to effectively create a multibrand environment, where we're marketing in a variety of ways and staking out different positions that enable us to be our own competition.

In fact, we've been a multibrand company since 1960. It was a very purposeful strategy on my father's part to say that if we're going to have competition, we might as well be our own best competitor. And so, we took the approach of slicing and dicing ideas and allowing each idea to grow into its own brand. That has turned out to be a very successful strategy.

Of course, we were also one of the first to open retail stores for beauty only. I drove us to become early adopters of the Internet and e-commerce as a meaningful vehicle for communication with the consumer. We were pioneers in business practices like gift with purchase, an idea first conceived by my grandmother, Mrs. Estée Lauder.

We haven't been the only company to make bold moves, but our competitors have often been content to let us take the initial risk, so we've led in many different areas.

As the leader of a global Fortune 500 company, how do you find time for your family and friends, and what is your advice to others when it comes to work-life balance?

It takes a commitment. When my kids were younger, as soon as we got the school calendar, I put every important date on my schedule. I tried my very best not to miss anything that was important to them or that I considered important.

Oftentimes, being there demanded what most sane people would consider a ridiculous travel schedule. But for me, that commitment to my kids was important. When you're older, you probably won't regret having missed a meeting, but you will regret having missed certain milestones for your family.

I consider my oldest and closest friends my family, too, so I make it a point to stay connected to them. I'm very proud to say that my best friend has been a friend of mine for over fifty years—we met when we were three. There are times when we'll go a month without seeing each other, but we always make an effort, and we know that we can pick up the phone and the other will be there.

There's no single rule to finding the right work-life balance, other than to say that if you don't take time for yourself and let your mind recharge, you ultimately will get burned out and not be as good at what you do.

How do you define success?

Are you happy? Did you take advantage of opportunities? Did you do the right thing?

If you can say yes, then you've been successful. It doesn't matter what the title is on your business card. To me, that's success.

But there is only one person who can judge your success—and that's you. There are people with a lot of money who are unhappy and people without a lot of money who are happy. There's no linear relationship.

The one thing you want to see in everybody is satisfaction. And I believe that you'll find great satisfaction in doing something that's not just about making money but that also brings you happiness. If you can find whatever that may be, and if you involve others in your enthusiasm, you will likely lead a happier life.

Do you have any other advice for young people who aspire to move up into positions of leadership?

Take responsibility.

Those who learn to lead are those who step into a void. I'm not saying it's natural in the sense that you have to be born with it—it can be learned. But it starts with recognizing the gap and asking what others think.

If you do that often enough, people will coalesce around your leadership. They will begin to look up to you and respect you. One of the main qualities we look for in a leader is the confidence and ability not only to speak your mind, but also to influence others through your words and actions.

Most large organizations also love young people who are willing to step up and accept an assignment. From a career-progression standpoint, those who volunteer and make an effort to do things that may not be popular—and those who take risks—are usually rewarded. That's especially true if they take advantage of the situation and demonstrate their ability to succeed.

If you look at examples of people who have achieved great success, many of them have not followed a traditional path. Not that a traditional path can't lead to success, but accumulating different experiences is a good way to distinguish yourself.

Finally, be curious. I can't emphasize enough that your learning should never stop. Learn from anybody and everybody. Read books, see movies, keep up with pop culture. Never stop being curious, because you don't know when the next great idea may hit you.

You often describe The Estée Lauder Companies as a learning organization. Why is that so important to the Company's future?

A learning organization is never comfortable in what it does. A learning organization recognizes that there is always uncertainty and insecurity, which require it to constantly question the way it operates.

In our organization, everybody has to continually reexamine their mission and ask: is what we're doing today going to be relevant to the consumer in the future? And what are the new ways of thinking and approaching our business that will allow us to evolve as a company?

Henry Ford, the founder of the Ford Motor Company, once famously said, "If I had asked my customers what they wanted, they would have said faster horses."

I use that as an example to show that, in addition to responding to consumers' desires, we also have to anticipate what they will demand in the future. When you think of the most transformative products, they were not typically things that the consumer imagined. They were products that somebody imagined they could deliver, and the consumer was blown away.

Another one of my favorite examples is the railroad industry. After World War II, the railroad companies defined their business as building railroads, as opposed to providing transportation. Even though there was this thing called an airplane that could transport larger numbers of people over longer distances at much greater speed, the railroad companies didn't think beyond wooden stays, metal rails, and big machines traveling along this fixed roadway. As a result, they missed an opportunity to maintain or enhance their relevance in transportation.

So, as a learning organization, we are focused on creating an environment that demands continuous learning and adaptation. It starts with having leaders who never stop exploring new ideas, and we expect that mindset to trickle down throughout the entire Company. We want employees to feel like they have permission to push the envelope and think differently, because we have to constantly reinvent ourselves, and innovation comes from every chair. Often the very best ideas are not those divined by senior management, but those created by people much closer to the consumer and to the process who see an opportunity and put their hand up and say, "Let's try it."

We're a different company today than we were twenty-five years ago. We were a different company twenty-five years ago than we were twenty-five years earlier. And I fully expect that twenty-five years from now, we'll be a different company than we are today.

What core capabilities will future leaders need to take the business to the next level of growth in the next twenty-five years?

The technical skills companies need will almost certainly change, but the core capabilities needed for effective leadership—curiosity, adaptability, communication, imagination—will be the same.

Leaders need curiosity to explore new areas, find new markets and new opportunities, follow their nose, follow a lead, and go investigate when somebody says, "You should see this."

They need adaptability to take advantage of those new opportunities and to recognize that just because we did it one way in the past doesn't mean that's going to be the right way to do it in the future. At ELC, we call this "learning agility"—the ability to anticipate change, face reality, draw conclusions, and swiftly mobilize to adapt to shifting needs and demands.

Effective leaders also need to have great people, and they're only going to be great if they are taught to be great. In the medical profession they call it "see one, do one." Watch a procedure once, then try it yourself with someone experienced looking over your shoulder to make sure you're doing it right. A manager and a leader are only as good as the weakest link in their chain. And if they've got someone who can't pull their weight, it's the leader's job to make them stronger. If they still can't, they need to be moved to a different place where they can be successful.

Finally, leaders have to be bold and have the courage to try something new. This applies both to their careers and to the business itself. I always tell my students, if you have the opportunity while you're young in your career to go live abroad and experience another culture or experience living in another part of the country, take it. Learn, explore, push yourself outside your comfort zone, as I did when I moved to Dallas for Macy's. It was an eye-opening and invaluable experience that I still draw on today.

And when it comes to our business, the next generation of leaders can't be afraid to take a risk. Our work is important, but at the end of the day, it's not life and death. So we shouldn't be afraid to be bold and try something new. Part of that confidence comes from knowing that you have permission to fail. Permission to fail entitles you to try to make it successful, and if it doesn't work out, learn from the failure so you don't make the same mistake twice.

The higher a leader climbs, the more their success depends on interpersonal skills rather than technical skills, because they are primarily working through others. Their job is to clearly articulate the mission and then guide and inspire others to execute it.

What do you hope to accomplish by the end of your career? What do you want your leadership legacy to be?

The most important thing I want to do is to help set our Company on a course for sustainable excellence and leadership in our sector that will last for many generations beyond the influence I might have as an individual. I hope that through the executives whose careers we've nurtured and developed, our Company will continue to adapt and thrive while maintaining the value systems that have allowed us to get where we are today—and that those values endure for many generations to come.

AFTERWORD

Arie de Geus, a longtime Shell Oil Company executive, author of
the book *The Living Company,* and father of the modern learning
organization, once wrote, "The ability to learn faster than competitors
may be the only sustainable competitive advantage." At The Estée
Lauder Companies, we know this to be true.

Year after year, we have enjoyed tremendous success thanks to
you—the extraordinary people who make up the Company—and your
insatiable appetite for learning. From our newest employees of the millennial generation to our most seasoned senior executives, our collective passion for learning runs wide and deep.

At The Estée Lauder Companies, we believe learning should be
a continuous exercise. For this reason, most of our initiatives in new
capabilities building have included an education component—and
many of these have been expertly supported through our longtime partnership with Wharton Executive Education.

Wharton Professor Patti Williams leads many of our executive-
education programs, including my Brand Equity and Business Sym-
posium. She has often shared that among all the companies she has
worked with—and there are many—our people are unique in the level of
interest, engagement, and passion for learning we bring to the classroom.

I know exactly what she means. I've seen it all across our organization, and I continue to learn from those around me today, just as I did
many years ago as a student in the Wharton classroom.

It is my hope that you, too, will continue learning at every stage of
your career and that this volume will serve as a valuable resource on
that journey.

To that end, on the pages that follow, you will find a checklist sum-
marizing the key lessons captured in this book—lessons you can draw

upon throughout your career, in moments of challenge and change, trial and triumph.

As many of you have heard me say, the secret to our success is great brands, great ideas, and great people. We simply could not achieve the results we have without the passion, dedication, and intellectual curiosity our employees bring to the office each and every day. You are our competitive advantage, and I am profoundly grateful for all that each of you do.

THE LEADERSHIP CHECKLIST

☑ INSPIRING EMPLOYEES TO ACTION

- Chinese philosopher Lao Tzu once said, "A good leader is he whom people revere. An evil leader is he whom people despise. A great leader is he of whom people say, 'We did it ourselves.'"

- Especially in large organizations with multiple businesses or brands, strong leaders must delegate not only responsibility, but also authority and ownership.

- To elicit the highest performance from employees, leaders need to foster a culture where each individual feels like the company's success is their own.

☑ SERVING STAKEHOLDERS, NOT JUST SHAREHOLDERS

- In order to effectively lead, C-level executives need to do more than answer to a bottom line and the shareholders who watch it. They must first fully understand the ecosystem around them, including the motivations, needs, and interests of all stakeholders.

- Shareholders are a meaningful portion of the stakeholder environment. But stakeholders also include employees, customers, suppliers, and the communities we serve.

- For large companies, this can mean a diverse and discon-nected collection of actors. But the extra effort of engaging stakeholders in decision making ultimately leads to greater value for all.

☑ MULTIPLYING YOUR EXPERTISE

- Great leaders are not content to be islands of excellence. They are teachers, mentors, and counselors, and they multiply themselves and their expertise by training their employees to perform at their highest levels.

- As a leader, your job is to teach others to be good at what they do so you can focus on what you need to do. The more people for whom you're responsible, the more people on whom you'll depend.

☑ ADAPTING TO CHANGE

- In a volatile world, leaders must be ready and able to adapt to change.

- The best leaders know how to change tack without changing terminus—to keep a company agile and flexible without losing sight of, or momentum toward, long-term strategic goals.

☑ OWNING THE MISSION

- Every single day, in companies the size of ours, there are millions of decisions being made. Of those millions, only a select few involve the direct input of the executive leadership team.

- The simple fact is, leaders can't be personally involved with every decision at every level of a large company. That's why it's critical for leaders to communicate a strong mission and a clear set of values that keep everybody on the team aligned.

- Organizations succeed when every member of the team feels ownership of the mission and understands the direction the company is headed.

- The job of a leader is to reinforce, enhance, challenge, and— when necessary—adapt the mission to changing circumstances.

☑ TAKING THE BIG SWINGS

- In the course of a career, there are a few decisions that every leader remembers. These few are the "big swings"—the important risks and big bets that change the trajectory of a company and an industry.

- The big swings are big for a reason—the value of their success is extraordinary, but the price of their failure can be equally devastating. So it should come as no surprise that big swings often encounter big resistance.

- Big swings happen in every industry, and it's up to leaders to trust their instincts, step up to the plate, and—with a little bit of luck—hit it out of the park.

☑ FOSTERING CREATIVITY

- Innovation and creativity come in many different forms and apply to more than just products and ideas.

- There is creativity in management and the way we work with people. There is creativity in experiences and the way we chart our careers. There is creativity in how we balance the demands of work and manage our personal lives.

- To fully unleash a great team's potential, leaders must foster a culture of creativity—in all its forms—by encouraging their employees to challenge the status quo, take risks, try new things, and not be afraid to fail in the process.

■ In this way, permission to fail is a crucial driver of innovation. It gives individuals the freedom to push boundaries and test and learn from their ideas—regardless of whether they are successful.

☑ LEADING TRANSFORMATION

■ In today's business environment, the only certainty is uncertainty. A great leader understands the nature of change and is able to adapt quickly to new realities—even when that means transforming a long-successful business model.

■ Leading transformation isn't easy. Humans, by our nature, are resistant to change. And generating buy-in is hardest when business is booming and a threat to the status quo seems distant.

■ That's why transformation is often best led in partnership between leaders who share a common vision.

■ It's also why crisis remains one of the best catalysts for change and why wise leaders never let a good crisis go to waste.

☑ MASTERING THE ART OF THE PIVOT

■ Many of the world's most beloved products are the results of failed experiments.

■ Recognizing when opportunity lies in a pivot is an important skill for leaders—especially those in creative industries.

■ Of course, not every failed experiment leads to innovation. Just as important as recognizing latent opportunity is the ability to differentiate between a business in need of course correction and a sinking ship. In the latter case, walking away is ultimately the right decision for the total enterprise.

- Good leaders are wise captains: they help their organizations chart the right course for success and use their unique insights and experience to adjust the sails when the winds inevitably change.

☑ PUTTING PEOPLE FIRST

- At the highest levels of leadership, EQ is as important as IQ. The best leaders know how to communicate effectively. They understand what motivates individuals and groups and moderate their approach to get the best results out of every individual.

- Good leaders build strong, well-balanced teams that leverage each individual's strengths.

- They also encourage and seek out team members who are comfortable speaking truth to power. A leader can't succeed by surrounding herself with yes-men and yes-women who only tell her what she wants to hear.

- At the end of the day, leadership is all about people, empowering them to build something greater than themselves, and enabling them to accurately say, "We did it on our own."

LEADER'S DISCUSSION GUIDE

"My hope is that in reading this book, and in absorbing its lessons of real-life leadership, you will feel inspired to explore and develop your own leadership style."

—WILLIAM P. LAUDER

This guide is designed to help you think more deeply about the multi-faceted role of the leader—and about the challenges and opportunities that you will face throughout your career, at every level of leadership within The Estée Lauder Companies.

The contents of this discussion guide are organized around the themes addressed in each chapter, beginning with William P. Lauder's Leadership in Action and continuing in order of the book's chapters. Each section contains a short list of Key Principles, followed by a series of Discussion Questions intended to spark conversation and personal reflection around their real-world application.

You may use your answers to these questions to track professional growth or to identify focus areas for further development. Discussion facilitators should feel free to modify questions as necessary to reflect the roles and responsibilities of participants.

LEADERSHIP IN ACTION

A *Conversation with* William P. Lauder

Key Principles

- Engage your stakeholders
- Multiply your expertise
- Learn from great leaders
- Do the right thing

Discussion Questions

1. The framework for William's Wharton class centers around two crucial aspects of decision making in the leadership chair: the need to consider many groups of stakeholders and how they are affected by your decisions, and the need to play many roles when doing this. In both making and implementing decisions, leaders face some of their greatest challenges when stakeholder interests do not align. Talk about a decision you've made that required you to weigh the competing interests of multiple stakeholders. What were the conflicting interests, how did you think about balancing them, and what did you do to manage the groups that were not entirely satisfied with your decision?

2. In a learning organization like ours, great leaders must also be great teachers. You possess knowledge that you learned from others and that you extended even further, and passing that knowledge to others is critical for us to continue to get better and better. In this book, William describes this skill as "multiplying your expertise"—the ability to train others to perform their jobs at the highest levels so that you can focus your attention

on the work only you can do. How much time do you devote to mentoring and developing others? How do you build that time into an already full schedule? What are the best opportunities for helping others learn within the context of your day-to-day responsibilities?

3. One of William's favorite principles comes from Lao Tzu: "A good leader is he whom people revere. An evil leader is he whom people despise. A great leader is he of whom people say, 'We did it ourselves.'" Who are the great leaders you have worked with in your career? How did they inspire you to "do it yourself," and what lessons can you take from their example?

4. William is fond of the saying, popularized by leadership scholar Warren Bennis, that: "Managers are people who do things right, and leaders are people who do the right thing." What is the difference between doing things right and doing the right thing? When in your career have you faced this tension, and what did you do?

THE ROLE OF THE CHIEF EXECUTIVE

Leadership Spotlight Fabrizio Freda; *A Conversation with* Nancy Koehn, Ph.D.

Key Principles

- Change begins with a clear vision, and with alignment around that vision

- Strategy is about choices, both in what we choose to do and what we choose not to do

- Start with a goal, then reverse engineer your success

- Use crisis as a catalyst for change

- Brilliant partners are better than lonely leaders

- Great leaders articulate a worthy mission, the larger context, and a role for each individual

Discussion Questions

1. According to Fabrizio, four elements must be a part of every strategic discussion: a clear vision; choices of where to play between the alternatives you have; choices of how to win in each of the areas where you have chosen to play; and a clear set of capabilities needed to achieve your goal. Share some examples of these elements from your team's strategy.

2. What vision guides your work? What are the underlying choices that have led you to that vision?

3. How have you aligned your team around a common vision? What can you do to reinforce that vision as you continue to move forward?

4. In this book, Fabrizio shares his belief that "the future of leadership is in brilliant partnerships, rather than lonely leaders." Have you experienced this kind of partnership in your career? How did both partners benefit? In your current role, who do you partner with to work through challenging decisions? How can you identify a great partner in the future?

MISSION

Leadership Spotlight Arthur O. Sulzberger, Jr.; *A Conversation with* Governor Jon M. Huntsman, Jr.; *A Conversation with* Alex Gorsky

Key Principles

- Organizations succeed when every member feels ownership of the mission

- Don't conflate staying true to the mission with sticking to a static course of action

- Leaders reinforce, enhance, challenge, and—when necessary—adapt the mission to new realities

- Lead with your heart, as well as with your head

- Make values a measured part of job performance

- Trust and transparency are the currency of leadership

Discussion Questions

1. Just as Johnson & Johnson relies on the Credo, the mission and values created by Mrs. Estée Lauder remain an important consideration for many of the decisions made at ELC. What role do ELC's mission and values play in your daily decision-making processes? Can you think of a time when the mission and values helped you to make a better decision in difficult circumstances?

2. What does "Bringing the Best to Everyone We Touch" mean to you?

3. How has ELC's mission changed over time? How has it remained the same?

4. Alex Gorsky has the Credo Challenge; Governor Huntsman gave out laminated cards. What tools and tactics might you use to ensure every member of your team feels ownership of the mission?

BIG SWINGS

Leadership Spotlight Edward D. Breen; *A Conversation with* Sarah Robb O'Hagan; *A Conversation with* Mellody Hobson

Key Principles

- In a crisis, triage threats and handle the biggest one first
- Leaders must be able to play the role of psychologist—if you do not understand the people you are leading, you can't influence them
- Never compromise your integrity—it's the one thing you can never get back
- Invest in your brand's core consumers
- Trust your instincts and make failure your fuel
- Take on big challenges one step at a time

Discussion Questions

1. When Ed Breen came in as the CEO of Tyco during the crisis, he identified eight stakeholder groups whose interests he needed to balance. Identify the groups that make up ELC's stakeholders. How do you think about prioritizing them, in your job and for the organization more broadly?

2. William and his guests often discuss what they have learned from instances of failure in their careers, and emphasize that some lessons are better learned from failure than success. Consider a professional failure you've experienced, at ELC or in another job. What did you learn and how did it change the way you approached the next challenge?

3. For employees within brands: Sarah Robb O'Hagan's turn-around of Gatorade refocused the brand on its core consumer, while expanding the potential market. Who is your core consumer? How might you challenge the status quo to compete in new categories? How do you balance entrepreneurship with staying true to the brand DNA?

INNOVATION

Leadership Spotlight **Lauren Zalaznick;** *A Conversation with*
Dr. Judith Rodin; *A Conversation with* **Jon M. Huntsman, Sr.**

Key Principles

- Innovation can come in all forms: product, process, and management
- Make innovation everyone's responsibility
- Create an environment where it's safe to fail
- If you're coming out with something new, be the first one on the block

Discussion Questions

1. According to Lauren Zalaznick, the most innovative companies make innovation every employee's responsibility. How are you and your team contributing to the culture of innovation at The Estée Lauder Companies, and how might you do so more in the future?

2. Lauren Zalaznick used a graphing technique to assess the relative risk and rewards of various innovations. How do you encourage experimentation in your area, while protecting your team from taking on too much risk?

3. Dr. Judith Rodin explained that resilient leaders allow space for safe failure, while taking steps to prevent catastrophe. A key safeguard is the capacity to self-regulate and quickly cut off what's failing before it becomes a substantial loss. What steps can you take to self-regulate as you experiment with innovation?

TRANSFORMATION

Leadership Spotlight **William Clay Ford, Jr.;** *A Conversation with* **Michael Eisner;** *A Conversation with* **Indra Nooyi**

Key Principles

- Always keep one eye on the horizon, even while business is good

- Find a partner who shares your vision

- Never let a good crisis go to waste

- Embrace change without sacrificing culture

Discussion Questions

1. Bill Ford anticipated growing concerns about fuel economy and innovation. Indra Nooyi saw changing consumer tastes. What trends do you see on the horizon today that could impact our business in the next five, ten, and twenty years? What can your team do now to be better prepared to take advantage of those opportunities?

2. If you were to start a company tomorrow that might be able to beat ELC at what you do, what would be different about your company? What can you do within your job to bring these changes to our organization?

3. We are living in the age of the empowered consumer. Today, we're experiencing a shift from traditional top-down brand design and marketing to a landscape of increased crowdsourcing and co-creation. How do you stay on top of these continuous changes? What can you do to stay better informed, and help your team adapt to changes as they arise?

THE ART OF THE PIVOT

Leadership Spotlight James D. Robinson, IV; *A Conversation with* Laura Alber

Key Principles

- Avoid the temptation to throw good money after bad
- Know when to course correct and when to abandon ship

- Blend creative instinct and analytics
- Encourage budding entrepreneurship at every level
- Act like an owner

Discussion Questions

1. Successful course correction requires that leaders maintain an impartial lens when evaluating their own investments. Jim Robinson suggests imposing rules in advance to prevent emotions from clouding judgment. Within your team, what rules do you currently use to evaluate the success of a project? What new ones might you develop to keep yourself and your team accountable? Even when rules have to be adapted, these conversations can lead to better decisions in the future.

2. Laura Alber led the charge to blend creative instinct with powerful analytics at Williams Sonoma. At ELC, we are also "creativity driven and consumer inspired." How do you think about integrating analytics into your creative work? What is the balance? Have you seen any inspiring models of this in other places?

3. Laura Alber's entrepreneurial advice to 'act like an owner' echoes Mr. Leonard Lauder's call to 'think like an owner' no matter where we sit in the Company. What does 'think like an owner' mean to you?

PEOPLE FIRST

Leadership Spotlight **Richard D. Parsons;** *A Conversation with* **Strauss Zelnick;** *A Conversation with* **Michael Berland**

Key Principles

- In a crisis, leaders define reality and give hope
- For a leader, "EQ"—emotional intelligence—is as important as IQ
- A leader should solve problems and clear obstacles for their team
- Don't chase your weaknesses; teams perform best when everyone plays to their strengths

Discussion Questions

1. An accomplished business executive and longtime member of The Estée Lauder Companies Board of Directors, Dick Parsons made a name for himself steering companies like Time Warner and Citigroup through crisis. He attributes his success to a simple insight: great leaders put people first. What does it mean to put people first? What happens when leaders get this wrong—when they make what seems to be the right choice, but don't invest time and effort in convincing people to execute it?

2. Along those lines, how have the leaders you've worked with earned your trust and inspired confidence—both in their leadership, and in your own abilities?

3. Michael Berland advises his employees to lean into their strengths, rather than try to solve for their weaknesses. How does your job align with your strengths? How do others on your team complement your skills and solve for your weaknesses? What can you do to help others around you build on their strengths?

4. Strauss Zelnick emphasizes that a leader's job is to serve their team, not the other way around. How do the leaders you work with serve you? How do they help you to do your job better? What do you wish they would do more—or less—of?